the comfortable home

an inspirational guide to
creating feel-good spaces

the comfortable home

Jane Burdon

RYLAND
PETERS
& SMALL
LONDON NEW YORK

4728953

To Anita Belfield,
with love and thanks

Designer Luana Gobbo
Senior editor Henrietta Heald
Picture research Emily Westlake
Production Gemma Moules
Art director Anne-Marie Bulat
Publishing director Alison Starling

First published in the United Kingdom in 2006
by Ryland Peters & Small
20–21 Jockey's Fields
London WC1R 4BW
www.rylandpeters.com
10 9 8 7 6 5 4 3 2 1

ISBN-10: 1-84597-151-5
ISBN-13: 978-1-84597-151-9

A CIP record for this book is available from
the British Library.

Printed and bound in China.

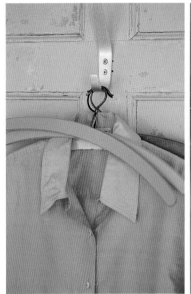

contents

COMFORT IS A MATTER OF TASTE

How do you sleep at night? Is your idea of heaven a soft mattress amid heaps of pillows or a firm bed made with minimal crisp white sheets? After a bath, do you dry off with a rough invigorating towel or wrap yourself in a soft chenille robe? Do you prefer to eat at the table every night or enjoy an occasional bowl of pasta on the sofa? Comfort is very much a matter of taste, and planning your home around personal preferences is more than mere indulgence.

Many interiors books and magazines focus solely on looks and lifestyle trends. While it is important to have a visually appealing environment, creating rooms that feel good is essential. A well-chosen mattress will help you to sleep better, for example, while a sofa that is too deep can only become a source of irritation and, possibly, back pain.

A home made up of good-quality, well-chosen components combined with tactile elements and accessories will make

Well-planned spaces that work in the way you wish them to work are calm and restful places to be.

you feel happier and healthier. This book will arm you with the knowledge to make informed choices, whether you are shopping for a dining table, a bathroom sink or a mattress.

A comfortable environment is about more than a squashy sofa or a soak in the bath. Well-thought-out spaces that work according to your needs are calmer and more restful places to be. We all need a place to eat, sleep, wash and relax, but there is no definitive template for living, so think carefully about the time you spend at home, your day-to-day tasks and the activities you enjoy. If you like reading in bed until the small hours, for example, a bedside lamp that casts a small directional light will avoid disturbing your sleeping partner. Plan your kitchen so that the sink, stove and fridge form an

imaginary triangle, and each element will always be within easy reach. Allow for additional stretches of worktop and perhaps a double sink if you enjoy cooking with a partner. Store ingredients and equipment you use every day between waist and shoulder height so that you won't constantly be stooping or stretching. In the bathroom, place a towel rail near the bath so that you can dry yourself immediately, and without leaving puddles on the floor.

Each chapter in this book covers a different space – be it for sleeping, bathing or dining – and begins by looking at key items, such as sofas, mattresses, dining tables and kitchen appliances, and how to get them right. Such items are not cheap, and you will be living with your decisions for a decade or more. The advice provided will take the lottery out of your choices and help you to get exactly what you want.

Once the essentials are in place, there are numerous other elements that contribute to a successful space. For example, versatile lighting that can offer at the flick of a switch both crisp clear illumination (for cooking, reading or washing) and a mellow ambience (for eating, lounging or bathing) helps enormously. So, too, does room temperature – if it is too hot, the room will feel stuffy and uncomfortable; if it is too cool, you won't really relax completely.

Many of us concentrate on the bigger picture when decorating and furnishing our houses, but everyday pleasures are often to be found in small details. Holding a fork that feels heavy and balanced, opening a door with a pleasing handle or stepping out of the shower to find a warm towel nearby all go a long way to bolstering mood. Our hectic lifestyles are filled with compromise and imperfections; finishing our homes with beautiful, tactile and well-thought-out fixtures and accessories will create an oasis of order and calm.

Many of us concentrate on the bigger picture – but everyday pleasures are often to be found in small details.

These days, most of our homes are shaped and styled with family life and casual entertaining in mind. Partition walls are commonly removed and doorways widened to create larger, lighter spaces. As far as room sizes go, bigger is definitely better. Such cavernous interiors are desirable when you have friends over, but they can make you feel a little lost when you want to enjoy a quiet night in. In spaces that feel too large, one solution is to mark out the central area with rugs and with lamps that cast pools of warm intimate light (avoid uplighters, since they will make the space look even loftier). Paint a wall or two in a warm shade that looks good in artificial light. Choose furniture with high backs, arms or headboards to make yourself feel cosier. Make a point of saying goodbye to armchairs, sofas and mattresses once they reach their tenth birthday, no matter how much you have loved them (make it sooner if they are showing signs of wear or are simply not giving you enough support).

The style of lighting can make or break a room. Combined kitchen and dining rooms in particular are prone to being excessively bright, which is both unrelaxing and unflattering. (Cheap restaurants use bright lighting to encourage diners

to finish their meal quickly and vacate the space for the next customers.) Avoid a single fitting in the centre of the ceiling, since this will cast the corners of the space in gloomy shadow, while the centre will look something like an interrogation room. Instead, install several light sources around the room, and fit dimmer switches for control. In kitchens, install brighter task lighting and softer ambient lights on separate circuits, so that you can tone down the lighting once it is no longer needed.

Clutter is the enemy of comfortable, calming spaces. Bedrooms, living and dining rooms should be clear spaces that allow you to relax. Hallways and other high-traffic areas need to be very accessible. You need to distinguish between useful belongings and junk. Piles of mail, extraneous side tables and broken tennis racquets simply don't make for comfortable surroundings (besides, if you haven't had the tennis racquet restrung by now, you probably never will). It feels refreshing and liberating to purge your home of rarely used appliances, clothes that don't fit or that are kept for sentimental reasons, and anything else you don't use but

are keeping 'just in case'. Paper clutter in the form of mail seems to multiply while your back is turned. Set up online facilities for dealing with bank accounts and to pay your bills, and avoid receiving countless letters in the first place. Place good-looking filing trays wherever post gets opened. If opened mail tends to get abandoned on kitchen surfaces or the dining-room table, reserve a nearby cupboard for stashing it until it is retrieved by its owner.

If your kitchen rubbish bin is constantly overflowing, buy a bigger one. If you recycle, allocate a specific space for each material, rather than let empty tins pile up on worktops, or newspapers and plastic bottles litter the floor. (If there is no space indoors, invest in a waist-height wooden garden store and place it beside the kitchen door.) If you find it difficult to let go, place all the items that you rarely use in boxes,

write on the date, and leave them in the loft or garage for six months. If you have not found it necessary to retrieve them in that time, you will know it is safe to say goodbye. It is not the end of the road for unwanted belongings; recycle, donate to charity, or hand them on to friends.

Ignore everyone else's idea of comfort and concentrate on your own. Home should be a personal sanctuary, a place where – if you so desire – towels are rough and exfoliating, and beds piled high with extremely unminimal cushions. Now is the time to stop imagining that you could do with a bigger sitting room or a larger garden in order to be comfortable. To achieve a comfortable home, what you need above all is a fertile imagination. The more you can visualize the details of what it would be like to live in a utopian environment, the greater chance you have of creating one.

relaxing spaces

ROOMS OF MANY PARTS

Most living rooms have multiple personalties. On some days they are sanctuaries for reading, watching television and chilling out. At other times they are dressed to impress and turned into spaces for entertaining. But a good-looking entertaining space should not be achieved at the expense of a comfortable private retreat.

Modern living rooms are often arranged with family life and entertaining in mind. Partition walls are commonly removed and doorways widened to create larger, lighter spaces that may combine sitting, dining and kitchen areas. Ideally, your living room should feel spacious and comfortable when everyone is at home but cosy when you are relaxing on your own. Place a favourite chair at a window or in a corner along with a good reading light. Fitted with castors, it could easily be moved to the centre of the room when you have a large gathering. If your space is open plan, mark out the sitting area with a generous rug and ambient lighting.

There is a balance to be struck between providing enough seating for guests and creating a living area that feels like a deserted furniture showroom. In a living room of average size, aim to seat four people comfortably (more if your family is large), and have extra seating for another four in reserve.

Additional seating in the form of a large footstool or an upholstered bench could double as a coffee table. Neat tub and slipper chairs can take up residence in an alcove or against a wall and be incorporated into the main seating arrangement when they are needed. If space is really tight, recruit your dining chairs (softened with padded seats) as extra guest seating.

A flexible lighting scheme can make a huge contribution to a living room's ambience. Place several light sources around the room, varying heights to add interest or to draw attention to an artwork or an architectural feature. Add uplighters to enlarge small spaces or use mellow table lamps to make big rooms more intimate. Whatever you choose, install dimmer switches so you can always enjoy the correct lighting levels, whether you are playing cards, watching television or chatting with friends.

Window treatments have an obvious impact on the style and comfort of the space. The eye is naturally drawn to windows, so curtains and blinds should frame views rather than hide them. During the day, draw curtains right back from the window and hoist blinds as high as possible to avoid blocking out any natural light.

While light-filled rooms are glorious, you may occasionally need to reduce lighting levels – bright sunshine can be very tiring for the eyes if you are reading, and its glare can make watching television difficult.

A combination of blinds and curtains should provide your windows with both flexibility and a well-dressed appearance. While slatted wooden or aluminium blinds might seem to be perfect for controlling light and glare, they are not the ideal solution for living rooms since they restrict the outdoor views.

Before you are tempted to reach for flimsy off-the-peg panels, remember that substantial curtains can block draughts and give living rooms a cosy, enveloped feel. If the room tends to get chilly, interlined curtains add warmth and insulation, and have a sumptuous weighty look.

sofas & armchairs

You will be living with a good sofa or armchair for ten years or more, so choose its shape carefully. Deep sofas with low arms and feather-filled cushions are heavenly if you like laid-back lounging but frustrating if you prefer to sit up straight and keep everything looking pristine. Tub chairs are neat and compact, and encourage you to keep your back straight; this might be ideal for reading but no good for lounging in.

To fulfil all your needs, opt for a selection of seating rather than the inflexible and often bulky traditional three-piece suite. Chaises longues and daybeds are often the subject

FAR LEFT *Large sofas with low arms and plump cushions are ideal for lounging on. Add a favourite pillow and a tactile throw to create the ultimate nesting spot.*

LEFT *Scatter cushions are more than decorative accessories. Choose good-quality feather pads and squeeze them into covers that are slightly too small.*

BELOW *Seat cushions made of feather are supremely comfortable but can look less than pristine after a couple of sittings. Choose feather if you are happy with a casual look and don't mind regular cushion plumping – or opt for foam pads and supplement with scatter cushions.*

of interior daydreams, but in reality they can be bulky and limiting in a seating plan. For a flexible alternative that can be repositioned at will, choose an armchair on castors with a matching footstool.

Take your time at the furniture store, and remove your outdoor clothes before trying out sofas that appeal to you. Don't have any reservations about sitting, lying, lounging and sprawling until you are happy with your choice.

A well-made frame will be heavy – while you are in the shop, try, with care, to lift the corner of the sofa to assess its weight. Patterns should line up, and the fronts of the cushions should match the remainder of the sofa; if they do not, you can assume that this shoddiness is replicated

elsewhere in the sofa's construction. Upholstery can hide many sins, and it is hard to judge a sofa's quality when you cannot inspect its insides.

There are a number of questions that you need to have answered by a sales assistant. For example, does the sofa have heavy-gauge seat springs? Such springs provide even and long-lasting support. (In high-quality sofas, the springs are individually hand-tied in place.) Avoid zigzag-shaped springs, which give insufficient, uneven support. Ask whether the frame is made from kiln-dried and knot-free hardwood. Kiln drying prevents warping and twisting, while knots represent points of weakness. Find out how the individual frame pieces are constructed. Dowels and glue are more durable than screws or nails. It is also good to know whether the cushions are lined. Lining reduces stress on the upholstery fabric and prevents feathers from escaping.

ABOVE LEFT *Tight-backed sofas – those upholstered without back cushions – are not for sprawling on, but they are good if you prefer to sit up straight for crafts such as knitting, or if you have back problems.*

ABOVE *Upholstered footstools and ottomans are supremely versatile; use them to put your feet up, rest books or magazines on, or as seating for guests.*

OPPOSITE *Sofas with removable, washable covers are the most practical choice for families with young children.*

BACK ISSUES

While the proportions, arm shape and cushion filling of your sofa and armchairs all play a part in the comfort of the furniture, it is the back that really sets the tone.

• **FIXED OR TIGHT BACK** A sprung back with no cushions to sink into provides good spinal support and encourages an upright position; a high-backed version also gives head and shoulder support.

• **ATTACHED BACK** Sofas and armchairs with cushions sewn onto the inside of the back are softer to sit on than tight-back ones, while maintaining a tidy appearance.

• **LOOSE-CUSHION BACK** A sofa with the same number of back and seat cushions offers extra softness; this style is often deeper than attached or fixed-back styles.

• **MULTI-CUSHION OR SCATTER BACK** Plenty of randomly arranged cushions give a casual look and can be arranged to suit people of varying heights and support needs.

BELOW LEFT *Wing-backed armchairs combine classic styling with a little privacy for the occupant. Well suited to a quiet corner, they are perfect for sitting in to read or enjoy a cosy, unobserved snooze.*

BELOW *Large spaces can sometimes feel too vast for genuine relaxation, but that is not the case in this room. The shapely sofa makes a dramatic statement, while its high arms create an enclosed and cosseting nest.*

Feather-filled cushions feel soft and luxurious and mould themselves to your body shape. They encourage you to sit deeper into the sofa and enjoy increased head support. The disadvantage of feather filling is the need for regular cushion plumping to maintain a sofa's appearance. Feather cushions gradually flatten and will in time need replacing or refilling.

Foam-filled cushions feel firmer than feather-filled ones and give more support for your back. The cushions maintain their shape and don't need to be plumped up. Check that 100 per cent high-density foam has been used to make your sofa, since poor-quality foam will begin to crumble within months. A foam core wrapped with a feather layer makes a good compromise. Combination cushions are softer than foam but need less plumping than feather.

Choose a sofa with a depth matching the length of your thigh, leaving a small gap behind the knees. (The gap lets you push back your feet back to stand up.) Your feet should rest on the floor without squashing your thighs or pushing your knees up. When sitting upright, your spine should form a natural S shape rather than a slouching C.

Armrests are often chosen purely for their looks, which ignores their purpose. When sitting, your arm should rest comfortably in a position that feels natural. If you like to lie on your sofa, choose a low, well-padded arm to rest your head on. For an intimate, cosseting feeling, opt for a high-sided tuxedo or Knole-style sofa. In smaller or enclosed spaces, a low arm will allow an uninterrupted view, making the area feel less cramped.

THIS PICTURE *If your home is open plan, try to be consistent in your style choices. Smart upholstered dining chairs echo a neat fitted-cover sofa in this apartment's living area.*

loose & fitted covers

Most people choose upholstery fabrics on the basis of their appearance or how easy they are to care for. Some opt for fabrics that are neutral or classic, so that they won't date too quickly. Only a few of us spend much time thinking about how the fabric will feel – but the 'stroke' factor can make all the difference between a run-of-the-mill seat and a favourite curling-up spot. For example, leather feels warm to the touch in the sun and deliciously cool in shade, while the nubbly textures of a jacquard weave can delight bare toes.

Before making a decision, consider the time of day when the furniture is likely to be used. For example, daytime sofas covered in pale cotton loose covers feel fresh and cool, while luxurious mohairs, velvets and silks are ideal for a bedroom chair or sofa that is used predominantly at night.

Loose covers offer great flexibility – and you can be more adventurous with fabric because it can be replaced when you tire of it. Odd pieces of furniture can also be made to match with the addition of loose covers in a uniform fabric.

By contrast, furniture with fitted covers, where all the fabric is fixed to the frame, tends to have a smarter, more tailored appearance. Fitted covers are not prone to sagging but they are difficult to clean and renovate, while loose covers are easily removed for dry-cleaning, washing or replacing. If machine-washing is a priority, look for covers that can be washed at a reasonably hot temperature (many manufacturers recommend only 30° or 40°C).

RIGHT *Almost-frilly loose covers give the sofa and armchairs in this loft-style flat a pretty, cloudlike appeal. Although the tailoring is subtle, the covers provide softness in an otherwise regimented room.*

INSET AND FAR RIGHT *Loose-covered furniture can be cleaned, repaired or made up in another fabric relatively easily.*

CARING FOR SOFT FURNISHINGS

While all upholstered furniture eventually comes to the end of its natural life, sofas and chairs that are well cared for will stay comfortable for longer.

- **KEEP FURNITURE ON THE LEVEL** Avoid warping or cracking by positioning sofas and chairs on a level floor. Replace any missing feet promptly (or remove them all).

- **AVOID STRONG LIGHT** Attempt to screen your pieces of furniture from excessive heat and strong sunlight, which may distort their frames.

- **PLUMP UP CUSHIONS** Regular plumping helps maintain shape and comfort; punch the cushions from all sides and drop them onto a clean floor.

- **ROTATE CUSHIONS OFTEN** Rotate cushions weekly to even out the effects of fading caused by wear and exposure to sunlight.

- **BE KIND** Don't perch on the arms of your sofas or chairs or allow children to bounce on the seats of upholstered furniture.

ABOVE *Sofas with fitted covers are distinctive for their smart, tailored appearance. The lines of the piece of furniture are crisper, and more interesting shapes can be created.*

coffee tables & side tables

A coffee table should be roughly two-thirds of the length of an accompanying sofa. A smaller table would look inadequate and would mean stretching to put down a cup or reach for a magazine. A table the same length as a sofa can crowd the area and obstruct traffic flow. While you should be able to place a cup on your table without effort, avoid feeling cramped by leaving at least 38 cm (15 in) between the table and the edge of the sofa.

Don't skimp on the size of side tables. They should be substantial enough to accommodate a lamp and any pictures or ornaments, as well as giving plenty of space to set down a teacup or a plate comfortably.

The ideal height for a coffee table depends on how you like to use it and the dimensions of other furniture in the room. A standard coffee table is around 40 cm (16 in) high, but if you like armchair suppers, a height of 64 cm (25 in) would be more useful. If you enjoy putting up your feet, you

BELOW LEFT Simple glass tables can be successfully teamed with various materials and styles. A glass table is a good choice for a small room since it visually 'disappears', helping to achieve a less cramped feel.

BELOW The height of a side table matters. Make sure that you can comfortably put down a glass or the television controls on your table as you sit. Choose a lamp and table combination carefully, so that light is cast at shoulder height while you read a book or talk with friends.

will need a table approximately the same height as your sofa (remember that you will sink into the sofa seat a little when you're sitting on it). Some tables can be as low as 28 cm (11 in), in keeping with low-slung modern furniture styles.

Side tables should be the same height as the arm of the adjacent chair or sofa (slightly higher for a very low arm). You should be able to place a cup or glass down easily. Console tables can 'ground' sofas that are placed in the middle of a room, and provide an excellent place for mood-setting table lamps. The table height should be level with the top of the sofa back.

THIS PAGE *Living-room tables need not be purely functional if there are alternative spots to place drinks, lamps or magazines. In this room, a simple side table displays a pair of treasured bowls. The table's delicate metal legs contrast well with the sturdy armchair alongside it.*

In general terms, if a table is the correct size and height, it will look good whatever its design. A contrast of materials or style can work beautifully. For example, glass-topped tables 'float' elegantly in front of sturdy sofas and give a feeling of spaciousness, while rough-hewn wood or slate make an excellent complement to lush chenille or velvet in a contemporary setting.

'Leggy' coffee tables look attractive against solid shapes, while a solid table would work well with furniture that has exposed legs. Oval and round shapes break up the gridlock of lines and squares that sofas and chairs can create. It is necessary to sound a note of caution here; however glamorous the table, don't buy it if there are sharp corners or edges – good looks are not worth the pain of repeatedly walking into a table at shin height.

Oversized footstools are becoming increasingly popular and are very versatile. Apart from letting you put up your feet when you want to relax, large footstools can double as both coffee tables and additional seating. A stool with loose or leather covers will maintain its looks, and one with castor feet will be easy to move around.

LEFT *Console tables can ground sofas placed in the middle of a room, disguise a less than lovely sofa back, and help to mark the edge of a sitting area. They also provide a surface for table lamps, whose ambient lighting can further define a space.*

FAR LEFT *A leggy wooden table works beautifully alongside a pair of long, low sofas. The slightly rustic style of the table softens the minimal feel of the seating.*

BELOW *Side tables need to be large enough to accommodate whatever you regularly put there. You should be able to put down your glass or book without having to take care to avoid other objects.*

lighting

Sitting areas need a mixture of mood-setting ambient light, for relaxing, chatting with friends and watching television, and task lighting for reading, writing or playing games. Lighting in sitting areas should also be supremely flexible to allow for the large number of activities that take place there and for changes in layout.

Avoid fixed or non-flexible lighting in favour of spotlights on tracks that can be moved and directed. Alternatively, align permanent spots with architectural details, such as the fireplace or in alcoves, instead of highlighting a sofa. Rather than wall-mounted lights, use freestanding uplighters to cast an ambient glow. Table and standard lamps can create light to read or relax with, and can be repositioned at will.

Well-placed accent lighting can show off favourite objects or artworks to best effect. Traditional picture lights are also available in contemporary designs. Choose one that covers the width of the artwork and that, once angled to avoid reflection or glare, covers the picture from top to bottom with an even light. Alternatively, small halogen spotlights can be angled towards an object. While you probably won't want to show off your television, watching it in the dark can cause eye strain. Place a lamp nearby to lessen the contrast between a bright television screen and a dark room.

Lighting looks seamless and inviting when it mirrors the decoration of a room. In general, warm yellow tungsten light looks best in classically styled rooms, while white halogen light complements modern interiors. However, halogen can create discreet accents in traditional rooms, and a tungsten bulb can add warmth to modern spaces. Use light as a decorative tool to create points of interest. Pools of light at different heights break up the strong horizontal bias created by sofas and chairs. A pair of table lamps will give an area symmetry, and a feeling of calm and order. Firelight and candlelight look warm, timeless and elegant in every space.

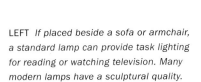

LEFT *If placed beside a sofa or armchair, a standard lamp can provide task lighting for reading or watching television. Many modern lamps have a sculptural quality.*

ABOVE *Control is the key to a successful lighting scheme. Fit dimmer switches wherever possible, so that you can alter light depending on where and what you are doing, or the time of day.*

ABOVE RIGHT *In general, central ceiling lights cast unflattering shadows and should be avoided, but period ceilings with roses can look awkward without a fitting, in which case a dimmer switch should be used, along with additional light sources.*

RIGHT *Symmetrically positioned wall-mounted lights give a sense of calm and order to this traditional fireplace. Small shades allow soft light to escape from top and bottom, echoing the flames of the fire.*

flooring

Your living room should be a place where you can kick off your shoes without a second thought, and – despite trends for hard surfaces – nothing can beat the feel of soft pure wool underfoot. If you dread having to deal with wine stains or pet hairs, opt for wood. Other hard surfaces may be ideal for a high-traffic kitchen or hallway, but living-room floors made of concrete, tiles or stone are cold and unwelcoming.

As well as being long-lasting, wooden floors are supremely practical and good-looking, and will give a contemporary feel to your room. Parquet or laminate strips can be laid, or original floorboards sanded or restored and refinished. A wooden floor is warmer than other hard flooring and has more 'give' (so it is not so hard on the legs). Pale wooden flooring reflects light into a room, while dark wooden floors can 'ground' an airy space. Since wood is relatively noisy underfoot, it is not always the most appropriate choice for flats or upstairs rooms. Another drawback is that rooms with wooden floors have a tendency to echo unless they have sufficient soft furnishings to counteract this.

Rugs can soften wooden floors, adding visual interest while creating a quieter and warmer surface. Large rugs can also be used as room dividers, marking out sitting or dining zones in open-plan areas.

Rugs can be cleaned, replaced or repositioned without effort or huge expense. On the whole, good-quality rugs are easier to clean than inexpensive ones.

OPPOSITE, LEFT *Textured carpet adds visual interest to a room and is supremely tactile underfoot. A good-quality underlay will ensure that the carpet is soft to walk on and will prolong its life.*

OPPOSITE, RIGHT *Laying the same carpet in every room helps to create a seamless transition between spaces. Uniform flooring in a fairly pale neutral shade will also give the impression of spaciousness, whatever the size of your home.*

LEFT *While wooden floors are not as soft underfoot as carpet, they are warmer and have slightly more 'give' than other hard floor coverings. They are also very practical and can be softened with the addition of area rugs.*

BELOW *Wooden floors are less vulnerable than carpet to damage by furniture legs or wheels. They can be refinished and revarnished, and luxurious underfloor heating can be fitted beneath them.*

THE CARPET FACTOR

Soft and luxurious underfoot, carpet has no real competition in the comfort stakes. Although it can stain easily and is less hygienic than wood, the advantages of carpet easily outweigh its disadvantages.

• PAMPER YOUR SENSES Carpet is warm and quiet underfoot.

• TAKE YOUR CHOICE It comes in many colours, patterns and textures.

• USE OPTICAL ILLUSION Wall-to-wall carpeting makes rooms look bigger.

• MAKE IT THICK The thicker the pile of your carpet, the more you will be tempted to sit on the floor.

• CHOOSE PURE WOOL Pure wool wears much better than synthetic alternatives and will not cause static shocks or carpet burns.

FINISHES

throws   Brightly coloured throws offer an excellent opportunity to introduce vibrancy into otherwise neutral living rooms. A plain or patterned throw can also be used to rescue a tired sofa and double as a blanket for afternoon snoozes. The fabric from which a throw is made is important; linen creases easily, while some wool textures can feel scratchy or itchy against bare skin.

rugs   Generously sized woollen rugs with a deep pile can be used to introduce warmth and texture into a living room and provide a soft landing for stockinged feet. Large area rugs also serve to mark out seating and relaxation zones. (Stay sure-footed by placing a non-slip mat beneath each of your rugs.)

cushions

Cushions have the effect of making seating feel and look far more comfortable. Scatter a casual assortment of cushions on your sofa and add a single plump cushion to each armchair. When additional seating is needed to accommodate guests, place generously sized cushions on dining chairs.

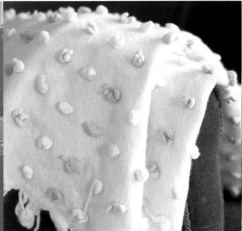

window treatments

Curtains and other window treatments in sitting areas should be regarded more seriously than as simply a decorative afterthought. Unless you live in the tropics, choose heavy lined curtains or weighty blinds that will keep draughts and winter chills at bay. Such treatments also serve to protect furniture and artworks from strong sunlight and keep living rooms cool in hot weather.

footstools

Footstools come in all shapes and sizes, and are supremely versatile. Use them to put your feet up while reading, as a surface from which to serve coffee or to create additional seating. A large, centrally placed, upholstered stool allows a sitter to face any direction to talk and offers a clear view across the room.

shelves & surfaces

Arrange books on shelves so that your favourites are within arm's reach (art and travel books are more likely to be thumbed through repeatedly than novels or biographies). Keepsakes give a beautiful personal touch to display surfaces, but the effect will be cluttered and hard to admire if you show too many items at once. Confine your display to a few favourite objects, rotating them if necessary. When deciding where to place objects, consider the impact at eye level both when seated, and when entering the room.

oversized style

When it comes to furnishing your living room for maximum comfort, big is definitely beautiful – and a room adorned with generously proportioned furniture and accessories can feel as warm and soothing as a hug. Choose plump, overstuffed chairs, plenty of fat cushions and large tufted area rugs to provide large quantities of luxury. Encourage lounging by installing a sofa that is ample enough to sprawl on with a friend. To avoid a sense of overload, restrict the number of pieces of furniture in the room and banish modestly sized pieces that may throw the proportions of the scheme off balance.

nature notes

A scheme inspired by nature that embraces tactile elements is a supremely livable look that will stand the test of time. Pale neutral schemes work brilliantly as a background for natural elements – as do leafy-green shades and darker neutrals such as coffee and chestnut brown. Enjoy combining wood, sisal and stone with linen, sheepskin or wool. You will find that – as long as you maintain a uniform colour palette – the more furniture styles you can incorporate into the room the merrier. A wicker-topped side table will sit very happily next to a whitewashed wooden chair or a soft linen-covered sofa.

soothing hues

Colours that you love will have an uplifting and welcoming
effect on you, so choose a favourite hue and go to town with
it. For an intimate, enveloping room, cover walls, sofas and
full-length curtains in a single colour. For a subtler approach,
and when dealing with vivid tones that could be overpowering
in large quantities, set colourful accessories against the
backdrop of a neutral interior. While many designers caution
against the use of excessively cool shades or stimulating
hues such as vibrant reds in sitting areas, well-loved colours
will relax you whatever their reputation.

cooking
& eating
spaces

THE HUB OF THE HOME

A comfortable kitchen is one that is supremely functional and user-friendly – a place probably used for eating as well as cooking, whose style and layout take many forms. Kitchens should be practical and streamlined, but they don't have to be clinical. Dining areas may have space for only a table and chairs, but there is no reason why they should look stark or canteen-like.

Preparing and sharing food is an intimate, enjoyable experience, and kitchens and dining areas should reflect and encourage this. These rooms should be a feast for all the senses, including sight – a rich wall colour such as deep red can create a cosy dining space and even stimulate the appetite. Copper saucepans are beautiful and can look decorative when hung from a rack. Glasses sparkle when placed in a glass-fronted cabinet near a light source.

Works of art and hot steamy kitchens don't mix, but plates and china can be mounted on walls to great effect in traditional kitchens.

A kitchen should be a pleasure for everyone to use. If two of you enjoy cooking together, a double sink and separate work surfaces will ensure that you don't get under each other's feet. Everyday cooking utensils and ingredients should be kept in places that no one has to reach up or stoop down to. Many mainstream designers are recognizing that appearance is not everything. Kitchen products that feel good and are easy to use are essential.

Good organization is crucial to efficiency. Regularly purge your cupboards of extraneous contents. Keep frequently used items between waist and shoulder height, and towards the front of cupboards so that you can see them easily.

Throw out anything that you don't use or place it on a high shelf. Once you have cleared the decks, use shelf dividers and racks to create a home for what's left. Large open spaces can become rather like black holes, but the smaller and more specific spaces you make, the more chance you will have of finding what you want.

Sideboards are making a comeback in dining areas. They offer a spot to set down serving dishes, and can store china and linens, freeing storage space in the kitchen. Sideboards also provide a space to display treasures and framed photographs, adding a personal touch.

Kitchens also need to sound right. A mixture of hard floors, worktops and cupboards can create an undesirable acoustic, which will be amplified by a lively dinner party. Soak up echoes by dressing windows with generously gathered curtains, adding a tablecloth or fitting fabric covers to dining chairs. For a modern look, have some fabric stretched over wooden frames to create acoustic-enhancing artworks.

The cost of fitted kitchens varies enormously, along with their quality. Many inexpensive, flat-packed units are relatively simple to assemble, look good and can perform their job adequately. However, they tend not to wear as well as higher-priced cupboards and lack 'feel-good' qualities such as smooth-running drawers and tactile handles. High-end kitchens come with an equally high price tag but they can usually be tailored to your exact specifications.

One possible compromise is to purchase cheap wall-mounted cupboards or to install simple open shelving to balance the cost of more expensive lower units and drawers.

tables & chairs

Sharing food with friends and family is a basic pleasure, and a well-proportioned table and comfortable chairs will make lunches and suppers all the more enjoyable. A well-made table will last indefinitely, so choose yours with care.

The size of your dining table may be restricted by room size. If you are considering buying an extendable table, make sure that the mechanism is easy to operate and that additional leaves are not too heavy or unwieldy. Remember that this is all about having guests over for a meal rather than taking part in an assault course! If you eat with friends regularly, aim for a table that can seat your immediate family comfortably, plus four more. If you tend to entertain more formally in a separate

FAR LEFT *Tables that can fold or extend are useful when space is tight – but, for large gatherings, nothing beats a generously proportioned permanent surface.*

LEFT *Dining chairs need not be identical. Mismatched wooden chairs sit happily together around a scrubbed pine table in this country kitchen.*

BELOW *Circular and oval tables can soften the effect of rooms filled with strong lines and angles. Rounded edges are also safer if you have small children.*

dining room, a small breakfast table could suffice in the kitchen. Whatever its size, make sure there is plenty of space around the table so that you can move freely. When choosing a table, scrutinize your dining area. For example, square tables fit neatly into corners, while rectangular ones can line a single wall effectively.

Avoid tables with badly positioned legs. Tables with pullout leaves or those with hinged sections supported by gatefold legs are among the worst culprits. While a table that can expand to accommodate extra guests is desirable, check that no one has to straddle a table leg as they eat. Ideally, the table should be wide enough for everyone to stretch their legs and relax after their supper.

Dining chairs should feel good no matter how long you sit in them. When trying out showroom models, pretend that you have had a couple of glasses of wine. Slouch and lean back as you might after a large supper. The chair should feel sturdy and weighty, but not so heavy that it is difficult to reposition. Even if you are buying a set of matching chairs and table, check that chairs match your table height, since not all companies get proportions right. (You should be able to rest your forearms comfortably on the table when sitting upright.) Padded or furnished chairs may be unnecessary (and impractical) for day-to-day dining, but are comfortable during longer meals and dinner parties. Loose covers that can be slipped over chairs when required are a perfect solution. Finally, avoid scraping noises as chairs are pulled back by fitting felt pads onto their feet.

Traditionally, only the 'carver' chairs at each end of a rectangular or oval table had arms, but there is no reason why every chair can't have armrests if you prefer them. Make sure the rests are at the right height for you and wide enough to prevent your arm slipping off.

Sometimes the way objects are arranged or contrasted can make you feel more grounded and comfortable. Chunky-style chairs can add weight to a table, preventing it from 'floating' in the middle of the room, while skinny-

LEFT *A diner-style banquette creates an intimate seating area, and makes good use of the allocated space.*

ABOVE *A pair of identical tables sit side by side, creating a single large surface.*

OPPOSITE, LEFT *Don't feel that you have to buy matching chairs with a new table. Many materials complement each other, as this sturdy wooden table and slender metal-framed chair demonstrate.*

OPPOSITE, ABOVE RIGHT *Tall stools in the kitchen are perfect for breakfasts, or for guests to chat to you as you prepare food.*

OPPOSITE, BELOW RIGHT *It is prudent to choose classic neutrals when investing in large and expensive pieces of furniture. But the golden rule is that you should love what you buy – so, if something funkier takes your eye, go for it!*

legged chairs can bring some light relief to rows of solid kitchen units. Other seating options for kitchens include bar stools and benches. A good stool should be easy to get onto and off, and have a well-positioned footrest so that your legs are not left dangling in mid-air when you are sitting. Stools with even a small back will probably be too tall to tuck under a work surface, but will be much more comfortable than a totally backless version. Benches accommodate several people in one sitting and can be stowed neatly under the dining table, but they are not comfortable enough for longer meals.

Cooking and dining areas are not purely for preparing meals and eating them. Sunny kitchens are the perfect spot to enjoy morning coffee. Guests often migrate there, and children often do their homework at the dining table, which you might want to supervise. If you have room, add one or two occasional armchairs or a window seat to create comfortable resting spots.

planning & layout

When it comes to creating or redesigning a kitchen, planning is everything. An architect, designer or builder (or all three) should be consulted in the early stages, but before you get bogged down in decisions about style and materials, ask yourself some questions about your ideal kitchen environment.

For example, would you spend more time in your kitchen if the space better suited your needs and habits? Do you cook alone or with your partner? If you share cooking, two worktops and a double sink would ease congestion. Do you have a pleasant view while using the sink or worktops? Perhaps you could change their positions to create a brighter outlook and enjoy increased daylight while you work. Do you have young children? If so, incorporate an area where they can play safely while you cook.

BELOW Whatever the size of your kitchen, arrange it so that the sink, cooker and refrigerator form the points of an imaginary triangle.

RIGHT A combined kitchen and dining area makes it easy to talk to guests while you are preparing dinner or watch over children as they eat. Trips to the table with hot food and piles of cutlery will also be quicker.

FAR RIGHT Treat yourself to a trolley. Trolleys have divested themselves of their 1950s 'hostess' image; use them for transporting ingredients or utensils wherever you need them.

THE SECRETS OF SUCCESS

Create an accurate scaled-down template of your kitchen and the large items in it, and experiment with alternative layouts.

• **PLAN AROUND AN IMAGINARY TRIANGLE** The sink, cooker and fridge should form the three point; don't place obstacles between them.

• **KEEP HANGING RACKS AWAY FROM COOKING AREAS** This will prevent pots and pans from becoming spattered with grease.

• **INSTALL WORK SURFACES ON EITHER SIDE OF THE STOVE** This will give you somewhere to put down hot dishes, pans, stirring spoons, and so on.

• **ILLUMINATE WORKTOPS, STOVE AND SINK AREAS** Avoid shadows by fitting spots or strip lights above and slightly in front of the person using the area.

• **PLACE ITEMS USUALLY USED TOGETHER NEAR EACH OTHER** For example, site the washing machine next to the dryer, and the dishwasher next to the sink.

• **ALLOW ENOUGH ROOM FOR DOORS AND DRAWERS** You should be able to open them fully without crashing into an open fridge or dishwasher.

• **PLACE WORKTOPS IN FRONT OF WINDOWS** This will provide you with maximum light (and a good view) while you are preparing food.

ATTENTION TO DETAIL

A well-functioning kitchen has many aspects, so consider the details as well as the bigger picture.

• **ADD SHELF DIVIDERS AND CUTLERY PARTITIONS** The smaller and more tailor-made each storage space is, the more chance you have to keep things in the right place. Some kitchen firms make adjustable systems to separate piles of plates, baking trays, etc.

• **ALLOW FOR PLENTY OF ELECTRICAL SOCKETS AND OUTLETS** This will enable you to avoid a build-up of countertop gadgets in one spot.

• **LEAVE OUT ONLY REGULARLY USED WORKTOP APPLIANCES** No matter how smart your appliances are, put them away when not in use.

• **CONSIDER INSTALLING GLASS-FRONTED CABINETS** They make it easier for visitors to spot a coffee mug or to find a wine glass, for example; guests who can help themselves will make your job as a host easier.

• **ALLOCATE A SHELF FOR COOKBOOKS** If you keep books in one place, they won't clutter up worktops.

• **MAKE ROOM FOR SPECIAL STORAGE** For example, if you have young children, include a toy box.

Start by making a paper plan or use a software design programme to map out your kitchen. Include the positions of existing waste outlets and water pipes for the dishwasher, washing machine and sink, plus radiators and power points. Most kitchen elements can be repositioned, but don't forget that you'll need to budget for the cost of alterations.

Do you prefer a built-in or freestanding kitchen? Fitted kitchens have reigned supreme since the 1950s, and recent developments include compact all-in-one units for people with limited space. But, as fitted kitchens become ever sleeker, freestanding units are growing popular among people who desire a less regimented, more organic look. Freestanding units can be mixed and matched, rearranged at will and taken with you when you leave.

Before taking any layout decisions, list the ways in which your existing space could be better used. Is the ratio of drawers to cupboards correct? Could china be moved to a dining-area sideboard or the washing machine placed in an outhouse? Also, consider your own habits. Do you like to display foods and gadgets or to keep them behind closed doors? If you are the sort of person who leaves the juicer or cookbooks on the work surface despite good intentions to tidy them away, it's better to go for wider worktops than constantly trying (and failing) to be neater than you are.

ABOVE *Chopping boards are never large enough – or in the right place. This butcher's block can be stored neatly behind a door and moved to wherever it is needed.*

FAR LEFT *Only one or two favourite appliances should be allowed to live on the worktop. Keep everything else in cupboards to avoid clutter.*

MAIN PICTURE *Fitted units create a sleek, contemporary look and maximize storage space. Doors that click open or shut with hand pressure suit a streamlined kitchen.*

LEFT *Arrange storage so that you can bring heavy objects such as saucepans to you, rather than having to scrabble about in the back of a cupboard to find them. Deep drawers near the work surface also reduce the need for frequent bending over.*

appliances

Appliances are meant to help rather than to irritate. If you need to operate numerous knobs and dials on a washing machine before you can start a programme, it will become a small but regular source of frustration. Whatever appliance you are buying, make sure it performs its function simply and effectively and is well insulated to reduce noise levels.

Be realistic about the size and type of cooker you choose. You may long for an Aga or a six-ringed unit with griddle, but there's no point having a cooker that takes up half a small kitchen if you are single and rarely cook. A double oven will allow different dishes to be prepared simultaneously; a model with a regular oven and a fan-assisted version is supremely versatile. Consider a wall-mounted cooker for greater comfort, especially if you have back problems.

Extractor fans remove smells and steam, and keep the room at a comfortable temperature while you cook. When choosing a fan, be aware of noise levels. Well-insulated

ABOVE *An extractor hood removes steam and cooking odours. If your kitchen doubles as a dining area, make sure that you choose a quiet model so that you won't have to raise your voice to be heard above it.*

LEFT *Range ovens look charming, can provide hot water and heating and often become a gathering point in a home. However, they are expensive and less than ideal for people who tend to cook quick meals.*

RIGHT *Cookers with six rings and two ovens are the stuff of dreams for many, but before investing in such a large item, be honest: would you actually use it all on a regular basis?*

models are more expensive, but bearing this cost is better than shouting over a noisier model while cooking for friends. The size and strength of fans are worked out by the size of a kitchen in cubic metres, along with the type and amount of cooking you do, so check with manufacturers before you buy.

Waste-disposal units mash up biodegradable matter and pass it through the sewage system. As well as reducing unpleasant odours in the kitchen, using a waste-disposal unit means that you fill your rubbish bags less often.

If you are installing a new sink, consider adding a water-filter system, which will eliminate the need for filter jugs in the fridge or stockpiles of bottled water. In hard-water areas, an integrated water softener will eliminate limescale build-up in appliances and make household cleaning far easier; you will need to install a separate tap that is connected to the water mains because softened water is not good to drink.

While they will never totally replace sinks, dishwashers have become a modern necessity. Remember who is in charge, though, and choose extra functions with care. Avoid dishwashers that beep repeatedly to let you know they have finished a cycle, particularly if you like to run the machine when you go to bed. However, a display that shows how many minutes are left to go on the cycle can be very useful. Keep a lookout for advances in technology. For example, it is now possible to buy energy-efficient dishwashers that

ABOVE LEFT *If your microwave is used principally for defrosting and reheating food, consider changing it for a smaller model. Compact microwaves can be put on a shelf to free up worktop space.*

LEFT *An American-style fridge allows you to store groceries that would otherwise take up shelf space elsewhere, so they are not always the space eaters you might imagine.*

OPPOSITE, LEFT *Dishwashers have become far more effective than they used to be at cleaning, and many use a fraction of the water that older models needed. This ingenious two-drawer model lets you fill one half while the other is already washing.*

consist of two pull-out drawers. The drawers can be used simultaneously or individually, so that there should always be somewhere to stack dirty dishes.

Can you fit all the groceries from a regular shop into your fridge without cramming the shelves? Can you see and reach everything? The top priority with fridge freezers is to buy one that's big enough. You will waste food (and money) if you have no room to freeze leftovers or if you forget about ingredients because they are squashed into a corner.

A trend for large, American-style fridges is catching on. Retro shapes and a wide range of colours mean that new-age fridges can stand tall. These larger-than-life designs won't take up as much space as you think; more food stored in them means less cupboard space will be needed. If work surfaces are limited, consider installing a fridge and a freezer side by side beneath a worktop. Buy a frost-free freezer: nobody wants to spend a Saturday afternoon chipping away at a melting slab of ice while wasting the freezer's contents. Fridges with glass fronts offer great views for busy chefs and wine connoisseurs. Slightly chilled drawers can be positioned below work surfaces to keep vegetables in a convenient place and at an optimum temperature.

RIGHT *Position your cooker and hob with care. If you allow a large area of work surface on both sides of the hob, it will give you plenty of room for setting down food after cooking, as well as space for utensils, ingredients and a few favourite appliances.*

sinks & taps

Sinks are an essential element of every kitchen and should be positioned so that they are always within easy reach. For efficiency, make sure your sink forms an imaginary triangle with your cooker and fridge, and avoid placing obstacles such as tables or islands in the central space between them.

Fashions for single or double sinks come and go, but your choice should depend upon who uses your kitchen and how often. If your dishwasher gobbles up most of the dirty dishes, you won't need to handwash very much and a single sink should suffice. Double sinks are extremely useful if there is no dishwasher, since china and glass can be washed in one sink, and then rinsed in the other. If two or three of you enjoy preparing a meal together, the chances are that someone will be washing salad while potatoes need to be drained. A double sink will avoid otherwise inevitable traffic jams.

If you regularly use a roasting tin, saucepan or chopping board that won't fit into an average dishwasher, choose a generous-sized sink, double or single, to accommodate it.

Whether your taps are traditional or contemporary in style, they should be easy to use and feel good in your hands. Levers are an excellent alternative to traditional taps if you have difficulty in twisting to tighten or loosen. They can also be operated simply with an elbow, which is ideal if you are working with floury hands. Taps with shower-type heads that can be pulled out to rinse around the sink are wonderfully useful, and some even come with a vegetable scrubber attachment. A tall-spouted tap (or traditional taps mounted a little higher on the wall) will mean that you can fill high vases or wash large pans without any problem.

OPPOSITE, LEFT *A double sink means that jobs such as draining vegetables and washing dishes can done simultaneously.*

OPPOSITE, RIGHT *Belfast sinks work as well in a functional modern space as in a more traditional country-style kitchen.*

ABOVE AND RIGHT *Mixer taps that include a pullout hose are fantastic for filling tall vases or rinsing out the sink. Whatever type of taps you choose, make sure they feel good in your hands as you use them.*

ABOVE RIGHT AND FAR RIGHT *Taps with a single tall movable spout give you plenty of room to wash a large baking tray or a bacon-juiced grill-pan; lever handles can be operated with an elbow.*

THIS PAGE *In addition to being glossy and glamorous, polished stone and marble surfaces are cool, which is ideal for making pastry.*

OPPOSITE, LEFT *Stainless-steel worktops can include integral sinks and drainage boards, reducing the number of joints and creating an almost seamless surface.*

OPPOSITE, RIGHT *While most wooden surfaces require regular maintenance in the form of oiling and scrubbing, they are hard-wearing and age beautifully.*

work surfaces

Worktops should be robust enough to withstand the effects of sharp blades and the heat of pots and pans, wide enough for food preparation, and the right height to avoid excessive reaching and stooping. If you can, install a long stretch of worktop, at least 90 cm (36 in), near the sink.

There are many different materials suitable for worktops. Marble, granite and slate are strong, hard-wearing and easy to clean, but they are very heavy and vulnerable to scratches. Wood is good-looking and warm to the touch, and it works well in traditional-style kitchens, but can be scored, marked or burned. Laminates come in a wide choice of colours and finishes and are cheaper than other surfaces. Resistant to stains and abrasions, they are generally low maintenance, but textured finishes, which can be harder to clean, should be avoided. Laminates lack the glamour of other surfaces, and can be scratched or scorched by knives and hot pans.

Stainless steel is hygienic and practical, heatproof and hardwearing. It has a contemporary appearance, and any scratches can add the appealing look of a professional kitchen. However, stainless-steel surfaces are generally custom-made, and therefore expensive, and they lose their showroom shine relatively quickly.

Stone composites consist of a combination of natural minerals and a high-performance acrylic, often finished to resemble marble or granite. Any seams or joins are invisible, and some surfaces have a slightly warmer feel than pure stone. Composites can be grooved to create a draining board or moulded to make an integral sink. But composites lack the glossy finish of polished granite or marble, and are equally vulnerable to scratches. Although cheaper than granite or marble, they need to be professionally installed, which makes installation costs higher.

flooring

Most of us choose kitchen flooring with looks, practicality and cost in mind, but there are other factors. If you like to pad around with bare feet, warm flooring or stone tiles with underfloor heating is an 'essential' indulgence. If you spend a lot of time standing to prepare food, avoid stone, concrete and ceramic surfaces, which can be hard on the legs.

Popular kitchen-floor materials include brick, terracotta and quarry tiles, which are cheap, hardwearing and warm-toned. Quarry tiles are less porous than other types of natural tile. Ceramic tiles are generally glazed, making them slippery when wet, and can chip or crack if a heavy object is dropped on them. Stone tiles – marble, granite, slate, limestone – are hard-wearing, water-resistant and cool in summer, but need underfloor heating in winter.

Wooden flooring is warmer and quieter than tiles or stone, and has more 'give'; it introduces an airy contemporary feel to a kitchen, and is long-lasting. If they are in good enough condition, original floorboards can be sanded and restored.

Wood must be sealed with wax or varnish for kitchen use. Linoleum (lino), a natural flooring made from linseed oil and wood flour, is softer and warmer underfoot than tiles or stone. Linoleum is an excellent choice for allergy sufferers, since it is made of natural materials that don't harbour dust or moisture. Vinyl – a manmade version of linoleum – comes in a huge range of colours and patterns. Easy to fit (it is very flexible), easy to clean and inexpensive, it is available in sheet or tile form. Vinyl can be laid on a slightly uneven floor surface, and its soft, slightly spongy backing has a comfortable 'give', though it is vulnerable to scorching.

Rubber is available in sheet or tile form, in a large range of colours and textures. It is waterproof, very hardwearing, soft, warm and quiet underfoot, and can be laid on a slightly uneven floor surface. Textured rubber floors are non-slip.

Cork tiles are inexpensive and easy to install, as well as being warm, soft and quiet underfoot; they can be sealed to make them more watertight, and come in several colours.

As well as being contemporary and stylish, 'poured floors' made of concrete, terrazzo or epoxy resin are self-levelling and come in almost any colour. Concrete can be hard and unforgiving on the legs and feet, especially if you are in the kitchen for long periods of time. Resin floors are softer underfoot than concrete or terrazzo.

OPPOSITE, LEFT *Wooden floors have a little 'give', making them easier on the legs than other hard flooring.*

OPPOSITE, RIGHT *Stone floor tiles are beautifully cool in summer, but chilly in winter.*

FAR LEFT *Linoleum is softer and warmer underfoot than tiles or stone.*

LEFT *Once a purely industrial material, rubber in tile or sheet form makes a durable, colourful and comfortable choice for the kitchen.*

lighting

Kitchens and dining areas need a mixture of task lighting (for preparing food, washing dishes and stirring saucepans) and softer ambient light (for eating and relaxing). Ideally, any new lighting should be installed before cabinets, worktops or appliances. Start by evaluating your present system. Is the dining area uncomfortably bright to eat in? Is there enough light to chop vegetables or weigh flour? Do you strain to see into deep cupboards?

We pay scant attention to natural light sources in kitchens. Windows are frequently underdressed, and wall-mounted cupboards can unintentionally block out light. To maximize natural light, add skylights or take windows down to floor level, have internal doors fully glazed, and dress windows with curtains or blinds that can be drawn clear of the panes. Avoid putting wall-mounted cabinets next to windows. Choose cabinets and worktops in pale, reflective materials.

Once a meal has been prepared, light levels should be reduced. Dimmer switches are extremely useful, offering control and flexibility. In contrast to bright task lighting, tungsten bulbs cast a warm glow. Use them in uplighters to wash walls in soft light, in standard lamps, or in table lamps placed on a sideboard or dresser.

Central ceiling lights are generally to be avoided because they leave corners in shadow. In a dining room however, this can be desirable; a pool of tungsten light centred above the table casts a warm and intimate glow. Chandeliers can add a touch of sparkly glamour, while adjustable pendant lights can be raised or lowered as desired.

RIGHT *A handsome pair of contemporary ceiling lights grace a smart dining area. Installing a dimmer switch will allow you to control the amount of light in accordance with the occasion and the time of day.*

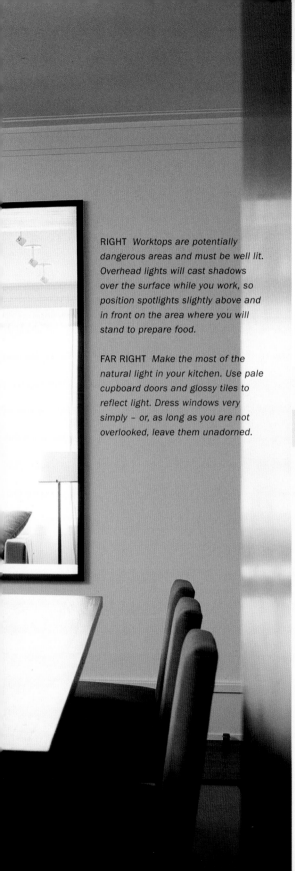

RIGHT *Worktops are potentially dangerous areas and must be well lit. Overhead lights will cast shadows over the surface while you work, so position spotlights slightly above and in front on the area where you will stand to prepare food.*

FAR RIGHT *Make the most of the natural light in your kitchen. Use pale cupboard doors and glossy tiles to reflect light. Dress windows very simply – or, as long as you are not overlooked, leave them unadorned.*

ILLUMINATING CUPBOARDS AND SURFACES

Well-placed task lighting creates kitchens that are both supremely functional and safe; without it, cooking can become a serious hazard.

• **BRIGHT LIGHTS** Place ample illumination in any area where you will be preparing food, handling sharp knives or stirring hot dishes.

• **SPOT LIGHTS** Halogen spots produce clean white light, and are perfect for worktops, sinks and stoves.

• **FLUORESCENT STRIPS** These now cast a vastly superior light to the bluish tinge of years ago and can be used instead of halogen spots. They are long-lasting and cast less shadow than other lights. They are also cool to the touch.

• **PERFECT POSITIONING** Install lights slightly above and in front of the area you will stand in to prepare food. (Your hands would cast a shadow over the area if the light source were directly overhead.)

• **DOOR-ACTIVATED LIGHTS** For a better view into deep cupboards, fit lights that are activated by the opening of the cupboard door.

• **UNDER-CABINET LIGHTS** Place lights for worktop areas beneath the wall-mounted cabinets above the worktops. Position them towards the front of the unit for optimum illumination.

• **SURFACE EFFECT** Dark granite or wood absorbs light while pale surfaces reflect it, so adjust light levels accordingly.

SUPER STORAGE

Well-planned storage means the difference between a highly efficient kitchen and cluttered chaos.

• **HEIGHT ALERT** To avoid reaching and stooping, store everyday items between waist and shoulder height, and towards the front of cupboards.

• **WITHIN REACH** Magic corners and 'round susans' allow you to reach all the items in a cupboard easily.

• **ON THE RACK** Use racks for storing baking trays.

• **EASY ACCESS** Store pans in deep drawers.

• **FRESH VEG** Store vegetables in open wire or wicker containers, so the air can circulate around them.

• **SAFETY FIRST** Place knives in an easy-to-reach knife block or on a magnetic wall-mounted panel.

• **HANG FREE** Keep open shelves and hanging racks away from greasy cooking areas.

• **STEP UP TO THE PLATE** Invest in a step stool and keep least-used items at the top of cupboards.

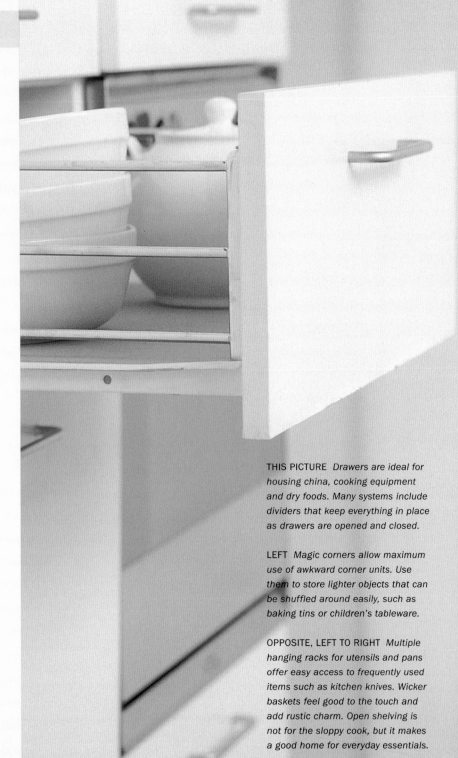

THIS PICTURE *Drawers are ideal for housing china, cooking equipment and dry foods. Many systems include dividers that keep everything in place as drawers are opened and closed.*

LEFT *Magic corners allow maximum use of awkward corner units. Use them to store lighter objects that can be shuffled around easily, such as baking tins or children's tableware.*

OPPOSITE, LEFT TO RIGHT *Multiple hanging racks for utensils and pans offer easy access to frequently used items such as kitchen knives. Wicker baskets feel good to the touch and add rustic charm. Open shelving is not for the sloppy cook, but it makes a good home for everyday essentials.*

storage

To create a calm and functional kitchen, you need to keep clutter under control. Shiny juicers and state-of-the-art food processors may look fabulous on the worktop, but they take up precious worktop space. If gadgets are not used at least every two days, relegate them to a cupboard. Make sure regularly used items can go in the dishwasher (you'll avoid piles of washing up). Every month or two, check the less regularly used ingredients lurking at the back of cupboards and throw away items that are past their best-by date.

If you are short of space, try to find alternative homes for items that don't need to be in the kitchen. For example, dinner-party china and linens could be housed in a dining-room sideboard, or you could move the washing machine and dryer to an outhouse or garage. To evaluate whether you are dividing storage space efficiently, reflect on your food-shopping habits. Do you shop daily, weekly or monthly? What proportion of your groceries consists of tinned or packaged/chilled/frozen food? Use your answers to work out how much cupboard, shelf or fridge space you need. If you tend to buy a lot of chilled food, for example, invest in a large fridge and have fewer cupboards.

If you require more storage space, consider installing drawers behind unit kick plates or simple MDF wall cabinets that stretch from floor to ceiling. Bear in mind that butcher's blocks can store utensils and vegetables, and those on castors can be wheeled anywhere.

FINISHES

personal touch

A supremely well-organized kitchen with clutter-free surfaces is one thing, but a cooking area devoid of personal touches will appear clinical and unwelcoming. Kitchens should incorporate elements that appeal to all the senses, and a large bowl of fruit or vegetables, a bunch of fresh flowers or a pot of home-grown herbs will help to create a relaxed, lived-in impression.

handles

Cupboard and door handles are usually chosen for their looks but, since they are touched throughout the day, they should also function well and feel good to use. Check that doors and cupboards will open easily with the handle you like; handles that are too small, skinny or polished may be difficult to grasp. Avoid ordering handles from a catalogue or on the internet; it is always better to try before you buy.

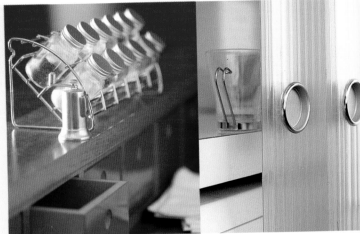

cutlery

Many of us are guilty of stashing away a glistening canteen of cutlery reserved for special occasions while paying scant attention to the quality of the knives and forks we use daily. All cutlery should feel comfortable and balanced in your hands. Choose substantial and slightly heavy stainless-steel pieces that will come to no harm if they are put in a dishwasher.

artwork

Chopping, seasoning and stirring takes time, and it seems a shame to have only bare walls and bland units to contemplate while you are preparing lunch or supper. Kitchens deserve artwork too, and a well-placed piece or two can blend the kitchen and dining areas together beautifully. If steam and grease are a concern, a collection of prettily patterned plates or platters on the wall would make an effective alternative.

window treatments

Windows should not be left undressed just because they are in the kitchen, unless you are deliberately trying to maximize light. Simple curtains will soften the harsh acoustics created by hard floors and surfaces. Pleated Roman blinds are particularly suitable near sinks and stoves since they can be drawn clear of soapsuds and sauce splashes.

daily linen

Good-quality table linen should be one of the pleasures of everyday life. Lay the supper table with large linen napkins that cover your lap when unfurled. Choose linen in plain white or a single favourite colour, or allow several shades to mingle. If you are lucky enough to own antique table linens, launder and enjoy them rather than stowing them away.

smells and flavours

Wake up to the smell of freshly brewed coffee – there is more to aesthetics than sleek surfaces and sophisticated worktop gadgets. A kitchen filled with the enticing aromas of coffee or herbs and with delicious fruits and vegetables on view will stimulate the appetite, improve your mood and give succour to the soul.

classic country

Contemporary lifestyles demand up-to-the-minute appliances and flexible entertaining spaces, but that doesn't mean that all kitchens and dining areas need to be clad in stainless steel and be full of sleek furniture. A classic country-style scheme can hide modern-day essentials behind closed doors and make you feel as though the day is long enough to enjoy reading the newspaper or chatting with a friend over a cup of coffee. Plate racks double as storage and display space for treasured china and kitchenware, while cupboard doors offer the perfect vehicle for warm, earthy colour.

softly softly

Kitchen and dining areas are hard-working, high-traffic areas, but that doesn't mean that they should lack creature comforts. While wooden floors and granite work surfaces are practical and beautiful, they can create harsh acoustics and their straight lines and corners can make rooms appear austere. Counterbalance hard surfaces with noise-absorbing curtains or a tablecloth, and cover dining chairs with comfortable padded fabric sheaths. The result will be a cosier space that feels more akin to other rooms in your home.

love the light

Kitchens are no longer dark little all-work-and-no-play rooms, and many of us now spend leisure time in open-plan cooking and eating areas. If you are a light junkie, maximize the natural light in kitchens and dining areas by incorporating light-reflecting finishes, such as pale paint colours, glossy ceramic tiles or shiny stainless steel. Many dining areas are configured with after-dark suppers in mind, but placing the table close to a natural light source will give a better outlook and provide better illuminated lunches.

sleeping spaces

PRIVATE SANCTUARIES

Bedrooms are often the last rooms in a home to get attention. We focus on fitted kitchens and chic sofas, rarely indulging ourselves by turning our bedrooms into the havens they ought to be.

These days, space is at a premium and we stretch our homes to fulfil all sorts of needs. Bedrooms may have to double as storage areas and home offices, but this does not make for a relaxing ambience. Sleeping environments affect sleep quality, which in turn affects physical and psychological states, so do all you can to cut clutter. Fit floor-to-ceiling blinds or curtains to hide computers and papers when you are not working and store little-used items out of sight.

Bedroom flooring should be soft, warm and cosseting; while hard flooring is modern and long-lasting, it doesn't match up to pure wool carpet or rugs in the comfort stakes. Carpet

is soft, insulating and quiet, and can excite your feet with delicious textures. If carpet is not for you, consider leather floor tiles. While leather is not as soft as carpet, it comes in warm natural tones and feels sensual underfoot.

Bedrooms that are both comfortable and functional require a mixture of task lighting (for applying make-up, dressing and reading) and ambient light (for relaxing). You can achieve this with dimmer switches and the careful placing of multiple light sources. Instead of unflattering overhead lights, install uplighters that wash walls with soft light. Choose large lampshades that eliminate the glare of exposed bulbs.

Reading lights on each side of the bed are essential. Make sure the lights can be used separately in case you want to sleep while your partner reads. Directional wall-mounted

or table lamps are perfect because they give enough light without disturbing your sleeping partner. Directional lamps are also useful for those who like to change position often while reading. If you choose a traditional table lamp, the top of its base should be at shoulder height when you sit up in bed so that you can read in comfort. The wider the base of the shade, the more light will be cast out and across the room.

Heating should be adaptable and simple to regulate. While cool, unstuffy rooms promote good sleep, most of us want to feel warm when undressing. After a night spent lying beneath a snug duvet, we also need a warm incentive to get out of bed in the morning. It is now possible to heat a home without any visible source, but fireplaces and radiators remain popular for a reason. Almost as much of a cue to our bodies

as the heat itself are visual signs of warmth. Working fireplaces are not often seen in today's bedrooms, but period and eye-catching modern radiators are very fashionable. If you suffer from a chilly bedroom in the mornings, place a small fan heater next to your bed, so that you can turn it on without having to get up first.

The bedroom is a place where you should be able to relax completely and be yourself, so don't allow trends or common sense to intrude while you are creating it. If you have always wanted an enormous leather headboard, go for it. If you enjoy listening to music in bed, treat yourself to a top-quality stereo. Fill the room with comfortable chairs, piles of cushions and trashy novels, if that is what gives you pleasure. Whatever you wish for, the bedroom is a place where dreams should be allowed to come true.

beds & mattresses

A bed is the single most important item you will purchase for your home. A comfortable bed will allow you to sleep well, helping you to face the world each day. Your bed is a place that should be whatever you desire – whether that is a cool minimalist haven or a nest that keeps you safe while you dream. On a functional level, your mattress should provide enough support to keep your back, shoulders, hips and neck in good alignment, so that you do not wake up with aches and pains. All this is quite a tall order for a single piece of furniture, especially for one that we spend a third of our lives in.

On the whole, the heavier you are, the firmer the bed you need, but weight should not be your only guide. If you feel that a mattress is too firm, it will be difficult to relax completely in bed. Above all, resist the temptation to buy a mattress that is a little harder than

THIS PICTURE *Creating and maintaining a clutter-free sleeping space will keep your mind clear, encouraging you to relax and fall asleep more easily. Store extraneous objects elsewhere in your home or invest in floor-to-ceiling storage. Remove computers and televisions from your bedroom, since they tend to stimulate rather than to calm.*

LEFT *Throw back your bed covers at the beginning of each day. This will allow moisture to evaporate, freshening bed linen and extending the life of your mattress.*

you prefer, expecting it to 'soften up'. A robust mattress will maintain its shape well and should not alter over time. Good mattresses are made of high-quality materials, both inside and out, so to a certain extent you can judge these books by their covers. However, while blue cotton ticking may give the impression of being French and romantic, don't let the outer layer be the deciding factor. Mattress covers should be well manufactured and durable, but their appearance is immaterial. Covered with a mattress protector and bed linen, you will hardly ever see a mattress cover, while you will live with the way the mattress feels for years.

Many of us choose beds that are too small, either through habit or in response to the size of our bedrooms. You should be able to move freely in bed without disturbing a sleeping partner. If you have small children, it's worth upgrading a bed size to accommodate sleepy night-time visitors. If space is the sticking point, look at repositioning furniture, reducing clutter or relocating wardrobes to another room.

If your bedstead is not a standard size, don't feel that you have to buy a mattress to fit it from the company that made the bed. Many firms will make mattresses to your size specifications at little extra cost.

OPPOSITE *Your bed should be big enough for you to move around without bumping into your partner. Also, if you have young children who visit during the night, a larger bed could give everyone more sleep.*

ABOVE *An ornately carved bedstead stands in a sparsely furnished bedroom. Complemented by a simple white duvet, the effect is Zen-like and almost spiritual.*

ABOVE RIGHT *If you and your partner have different views on mattresses, think about two single beds that zip together, each with a different specification.*

Consider the combined height of the base and mattress before you choose a bed. If you dream of a lofty platform, plump for a long-legged metal base or divan, or, if you prefer to edge out of bed slowly in the morning, select a low wooden base. Whatever a bed's height, you should be able to get in and out of it without effort.

Many traditional mattresses need to be turned regularly to help the upholstery fillings settle down and to ensure even wear and tear. Good-quality mattresses are heavy and unwieldy, so if limited space in your bedroom would make this difficult, look for a mattress that does not need to be turned. Single beds that zip together are much easier to handle if turning is a problem, and are a good solution for sleeping partners with differing mattress preferences.

If your mattress is more than ten years old, it is time to replace it. Other signs that you need a new mattress include regularly waking up with aches and pains, and sleeping better in beds other than your own. If you can feel springs or ridges beneath the surface, or if you and your partner roll towards each other unintentionally, it is also time to say goodbye to your mattress. If replacing your mattress is not an option, feather beds offer an instant and luxurious upgrade. Effectively a duvet placed on top of an existing mattress, feather beds can soften the blow of mattresses that are too hard or suffer from wayward springs.

Price tags generally indicate quality, so buy the most expensive mattress you can afford. For traditional sprung mattresses, ask the sales assistant to tell you the number of coils per square foot of mattress; the greater the concentration of coils, the better and more durable the mattress. Another thing to check is the length of warranty; generally, the longer the warranty, the higher the quality of materials and workmanship will be.

When you buy a new mattress, it pays to sleep on it for about six months, even if you bought it for use in a guest bedroom. That way, any flaws will be evident and you can correct them while the mattress is still under guarantee.

Once you have found your perfect mattress, there are plenty of ways to maintain a long-lasting relationship with it.

• **COVER IT UP** Use a washable, protective cover to keep the mattress in good condition.

• **ALLOW IT TO BREATHE** Throw back the bed covers for 20 minutes each morning to 'air' the mattress and let moisture evaporate. Avoid waterproof sheets or coverings that prevent the mattress from breathing.

• **AVOID DAMAGE TO SPRING COILS** On slat-based beds, make sure that the gap between slats is around 25 mm (1 in) or less to avoid damage to spring-coil mattresses.

• **TURN IT REGULARLY** Turn your mattress from side to side and end to end every few months (every week for the first three months) to help the upholstery fillings to settle down evenly.

• **TREAT WITH CARE** Avoid sitting on the edge of the bed and don't allow your children to bounce on it.

• **DON'T SQUASH IT** If possible, avoid squashing your mattress to store or transport it – it may never recover.

• **USE THE HANDLES** Mattress handles are there to help you position the mattress on its base – don't try to lift the whole mattress with them.

• **VACUUM THE MATTRESS AND BASE REGULARLY** Use mild detergent and warm or cold water on stains but don't soak them.

FAR LEFT *Mattresses are sometimes attractively covered in silky fabrics or French ticking. While this is often a sign of quality, don't allow yourself to be swayed by appearances alone; you will rarely see your mattress once it is covered in bed linen.*

LEFT *A feather bed (a duvet-like covering that you lie on top of) can extend the life of a tired mattress or make an over-firm mattress more comfortable. Many people sleep on a feather bed during the winter for additional warmth and cosiness.*

duvets

There is nothing wrong with traditional sheets and blankets, but they don't come close to a duvet. A quilt is a grown-up comfort blanket, and should encourage you to relax and sleep deeply. Rather than settle for the first one you can find, take time to consider your preferences.

Most duvets are given a tog rating, which indicates their warmth in terms of thermal resistance. A lightweight, 4.5-tog duvet is considered suitable for summer use; a medium, 10.5-tog quilt works well during the spring and autumn; while a heftier, 13.5-tog cover should keep you warm in winter. Combination sets of 9-tog and 4.5-tog duvets can be used

either separately or snapped together, depending on the season. These recommendations are supposed to relate to the average person; there is nothing to stop you going for a lighter or heavier cover than the guidelines suggest.

If you want to avoid late-night tussles with your sleeping partner, choose a generous-sized duvet. Your quilt should be at least 45 cm (18 in) wider than your mattress, so opt for a duvet that's a size bigger than the bed (for example, a queen-sized duvet for a regular double bed). Using an oversized duvet will also make the bed look fuller and more inviting. If you and your parther both like to have lots of duvet or have different preferences when it comes to tog-rating, consider investing in a quilt for each of you.

OPPOSITE, LEFT *Duvets are graded in 'togs'. In summer, choose a low 4.5 togs, in winter a hefty 13.5 togs, and 10.5 togs for other times.*

OPPOSITE, RIGHT *Duvet shells should be made of breathable fabric that has a high thread count to* prevent straying feathers, and strong stitched panels so that fillings do not bunch together.

THIS PAGE *Silk duvets look sleek and drape well. They are also lightweight, warm and an excellent alternative to down for those with an allergy.*

RIGHT *Since different seasons call for warmer or lighter coverings, some manufacturers offer combination duvets, consisting of a thin summer cover and a detachable middleweight version that together create a winter duvet. If you prefer a consistently lighter cover, look for single duvets that can be fastened together.*

FAR RIGHT *A duvet that's a size bigger than your bed will look full and generous by day and give two of you plenty of cover while you are asleep.*

CHOOSING YOUR IDEAL DUVET

- **WEIGHTY AND WARM** Wool duvets are for those who like weight and many of them suit allergy sufferers. Wool's breathable and insulating qualities regulate body temperature. These quilts are classed by weight per metre, but ask a sales assistant for their tog equivalent.

- **WEIGHTY BUT NOT TOO WARM** If you like weight but want to keep cool, choose cotton, a breathable, long-lasting material that is also machine-washable. Duvets are usually around 6 to 7 togs.

- **LIGHTWEIGHT AND WARM** Pure down or down-and-feather mix duvets are for those seeking warmth without weight. The higher the down content, the softer, lighter and costlier the duvet will be. Goose down is more expensive than duck, but is lighter, softer and gives more warmth. Siberian and Hungarian goose down is warmer, lighter, softer – and more expensive still.

- **LIGHTWEIGHT AND SLEEK** Silk duvets are lighter than feather ones and drape well. Silk can absorb almost 30 per cent of its weight in moisture without feeling damp, making silk duvets warm in winter and cool in summer. Silk can soothe itchy skin; many duvets suit allergy sufferers.

- **WARM AND HYPOALLERGENIC** Synthetic fillings are warm, light, machine-washable and perfect for anyone who is allergic to feathers or down. These fillings tend not to mould themselves around your body as well as down, so buy a larger size to allow plenty of cover to snuggle into.

Natural fillings are soft and warm, and duvets made from them mould themselves around the shape of the sleeper; they are also highly resilient and tend to last longer than their synthetic counterparts. However, synthetic fillings are an excellent choice for allergy sufferers; they are less expensive than down and are easy to launder in a washing machine. Don't discount either until you've had a chance to examine both closely.

Duvet casings should be made of strong breathable fabric. Check for sturdy stitching that will prevent channels and pockets merging to create lumps or cold spots. The thread count of the casing fabric should be at least 230 to prevent feathers and down from escaping. (The thread count is the number of horizontal and vertical threads per square inch of fabric.)

Duck down and synthetic materials both make good duvet fillings, but there are several alternatives worth exploring. While your nearest high street may not stock every option, explore what's available on the internet or travel a little further afield. It is worth going the extra distance for a good night's sleep.

pillows

Representing a lot more than simply a soft spot on which to lay your head, a pillow should work hard at night to keep your neck and back in healthy alignment. It is preferable to sleep with a single pillow. (If you are using two or more, the chances are that your pillows are not the right density for you – and you may be waking up with aches and pains.)

The density of your pillow should not be a matter of purely personal preference. Use your regular sleeping position to gauge the level of support you really need. If you sleep on your front or move around frequently during the night, choose a soft pillow. Light support will prevent back and neck strain. If you usually sleep on your side, you will need a firm pillow to fill the large gap between your head and the mattress. A firm pillow needn't feel hard; many are composed of a dense core covered with a softer layer for comfort. If you lie flat on your back at night, choose a medium-density pillow.

Most people keep their pillows for far too long. Down-filled pillows last around five years; synthetic fillings last between six months and two years; wool and cotton last around three years. If your pillow is past its sell-by date, let it go. Fold your pillow in half – then release it. Does it jump back into shape quickly? If not, dispose of it. A good pillow should conform to your natural contours and provide support for your head. If your head and shoulders don't feel properly aligned and comfortable, get rid of the pillow.

Regular rectangular pillows are best for sleeping, but pillows come in all shapes and sizes for reading, relaxing and creating a comfortable-looking bed. Large square or

LEFT *Compensate for hard metal bedsteads with a pile of soft pillows.*

OPPOSITE, BELOW LEFT AND ABOVE *Bolster pillows provide very good neck support while you are sitting up or reading in bed. They are also wonderful for placing under the knees if you like sleeping on your back; masseurs often give their clients this comfortable support during treatments.*

OPPOSITE, BELOW RIGHT *No matter how pretty its cover, a down pillow needs to be replaced every five years or so. Fold your pillow in half and let it go. If it doesn't bounce back into shape straightaway, replace it.*

king-sized rectangular pillows look inviting on the bed atop regular pillows (particularly in contrasting bed linen), and provide additional support when you need it for reading.

Even if you prefer feather pillows to sleep on, synthetic fillings are a satisfactory choice for reading pillows, since they tend to keep their shape well; V–shaped pillows also provide excellent support while reading. If you are pregnant (or just love to cuddle up at night), hugging an extra-long rectangular pillow will give support and comfort. People with neck and back problems need specialist treatment and advice on pillows – but, for a simple 'stiff neck', exchanging your pillow for one that's a little firmer or softer than you normally use can help considerably. Try to keep a variety of guest 'spares' in your linen cupboard.

While you need only a single pillow to rest your head on, multiple pillows also have a role. Cushions and bolsters create a relaxing atmosphere, and are great for lounging. Pile the bed high with a scattering of tiny square boudoir pillows, either covered in a single shade or a chocolate-box assortment of contrasting fabrics and textures. Alternatively, bolster pillows offer a crisper, grown-up style, and come in several sizes. They also make very effective neck supports and are particularly useful when you are sitting up in bed.

Pillows should be laundered or dry-cleaned annually. Wash them in cold water, using a detergent that contains a degreaser, to remove oils. Tumble-dry pillows individually on the lowest setting; place a tennis ball with the pillow so that the filling moves as it dries. Store pillows in a dry and well-ventilated cupboard or room when not in use. Always use a protective cover underneath the pillowcase.

BUYING SOFT, LONG-LASTING, COTTON BED LINEN

- **THREAD COUNT** Choose bed linen with a thread count of at least 180. The thread count is the number of horizontal and vertical threads per square inch of fabric. Look out for the terms 'percale' or 'Egyptian cotton', which denote a count of 180 or over.

- **STAPLES** Sheets woven from long cotton fibres or 'staples' are noticeably softer than those made from shorter fibres. Also, the fabric won't pill or lint like bed linen made from shorter fibres. Look out for the terms 'Egyptian cotton', 'Pima', 'Supima' and 'Sea Island', all of which denote high-quality long fibres.

- **COMBED AND MERCERIZED** Cotton used to make the linen should be 'combed and mercerized'; this swells the fibres to produce the softest of sheets.

bed linen

After investing in a good mattress, supportive pillows and a luxurious duvet, bed linen may seem merely a decorative finishing touch – but, since sheets and duvets make direct skin contact, they should feel far better than they look.

Silk evokes silver-screen glamour, but give it a miss unless you like slipping about in bed. Polyester sheets and cotton/synthetic blends are easy to iron, but they feel awful and leave you hot and clammy. Linen is cool and comfortable but can be a bit rough; it also creases badly. In truth, nothing

LEFT AND OPPOSITE Pure cotton bed linen with a high thread count is easy to take care of, feels lovely against bare skin and will stay in good condition for many years.

THIS PICTURE Coloured bed linen is usually dyed after it has been sewn, which gives it a slightly stiff feel. For softness, choose good-quality, pure-white bed linen and spice it up with brightly coloured cushions and throws.

beats the feel of freshly laundered, pure cotton white sheets. Cotton bed linen wicks away excess moisture, keeping the sleeper dry and comfortable. Cotton can also be washed at high settings and releases dirt easily when wet, so cotton bed linen will stay in good shape for years.

Hang your sheets outdoors to dry whenever you can. It is impossible to replicate a glorious 'fresh air' scent with fragranced conditioners or laundry liquid.

THIS PAGE AND OPPOSITE *Guests don't always feel comfortable asking for additional bedding, so leave a stack of extra covers and pillows on a spot where they will easily be seen. Furnish a guest room with the same comforts you enjoy in your own room. Think of your own relaxation, too; a little forward planning will mean you can enjoy the company of your guests, rather than running around in search of clean sheets and pillowcases.*

guest rooms

Making visitors feel welcome is a host's most crucial role, but hospitality is about more than simply saying, 'Make yourself at home.' One common error in spare bedrooms is to fill them with cast-offs. Guests won't enjoy sleeping with lumpy pillows or a patchy duvet any more than you would.

The best way to find out whether your spare room passes muster is to spend a night in it yourself. Make a note of what you miss – an alarm clock, a dressing table or a dressing gown, for instance. Are the bedside lamps too dim for reading? Is the wall colour bright and unrelaxing?

Spare rooms often have to double as storage areas, home offices or playrooms, but sleeping in chaotic or overcrowded spaces is not pleasant. Find a way of de-cluttering when you have visitors. A pretty folding screen will hide toys, while floor-to-ceiling curtains or blinds could disguise a work area. If space allows, fit large floor-to-ceiling cupboards so that you can close the doors on your clutter.

Sofa beds are a popular choice in homes that lack a spare bedroom, but they have drawbacks. A mattress that spends most of its life squashed, folded and sat upon will never be as comfortable as one that lies flat, and most sofa beds are not as soft to sit on as regular couches. If you decide on a sofa bed, inspect the bed mechanism thoroughly before you buy and choose the best quality you can afford.

Inflatable mattresses are relatively cheap and compact to store. Some mattresses self-inflate quickly, and most have a plush covering that stops bed linen slipping around. If you don't have enough floor space for an inflatable mattress, place one on top of your sofa-bed frame for extra comfort.

Rather than rushing around at the last minute to launder sheets or find a missing pillowcase, have plenty of bed linen to hand. Aim to have three sets for each bed in your home. That way, you can have a set on the bed, one in the laundry and another in the linen cupboard.

WAYS TO MAKE YOUR GUESTS FEEL SPECIAL

If you treat a guest room as if it were your own bedroom, you won't go far wrong.

• **BOOKS** Put a few carefully chosen books and magazines on bedside tables.

• **DRINKING WATER** If you don't possess a water carafe, a tumbler placed over a pretty glass jar or a bottle looks just as good.

• **TOWEL RAIL** Avoid piles of damp towels by installing a towel rail in the bedroom.

• **MIRROR** Guests will find a well-lit mirror useful. A mirror in the bedroom may also help to avoid bathroom congestion.

• **RADIO** Many people like waking up to the radio. If you install a clock radio in the room, you won't have to scrabble around for an alarm clock when guests need to be woken in the morning.

• **BLANKETS** It's miserable to feel chilly in bed. Leave a pile of extra blankets or throws where guests can easily find them.

• **PEG RAIL** A wall-mounted wooden peg rail or a multi-pronged hook on the back of the door should be ample to hang clothes.

• **HAIRDRYER** A hairdryer will be appreciated by visitors, who may not want to ask you if they can borrow one.

FINISHES

chairs

A comfortable chair provides a secluded spot for reading or winding down at the end of the day, and transforms a simple bedroom into a boudoir. Treat yourself to indulgent fabrics that are too high-risk in child-friendly or high-traffic areas of your home. Sumptuous velvets, shot silk and tactile textures all work beautifully in bedrooms.

cushions

Scatter cushions are more than mere decorative extras. Large square cushions and V-shaped pillows are both excellent for added comfort when you are reading in bed, while bolster-shaped cushions can provide support for the neck or lower back. A plump cushion makes a good resting spot for a breakfast tray or a book.

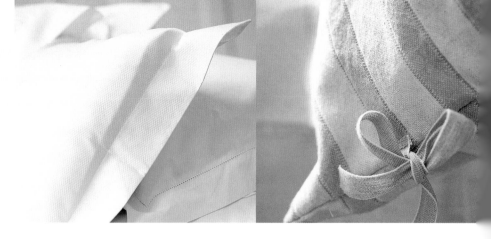

headboards

Wrought-iron headboards are beautiful and romantic, but uncomfortable to lean against without lots of pillows. Sleek contemporary designs offer cutting-edge style, and often sharp corners to match. If you enjoy reading in bed, choose a soft padded headboard that is securely attached to the bed base.

tables   Choose bedside tables that match the height of your bed – you should be able to set down a glass of water easily while sitting in bed. Tables should also be large enough to accommodate your bedside paraphernalia without a squeeze. Avoid painful bumps in the night by choosing circular tables or ones with rounded corners.

curtains   When deciding on window treatments in a bedroom, take into account of how much privacy you require and the amount of light you like to be greeted by each morning. Sheer drapes provide soft diffused light – an early morning wake-up call – and will allow you to make the most of a great view. Heavy lined curtains will muffle outside noises, insulate the room and block out large quantities of light.

music   Many of us fill our bedrooms with televisions and computer games that overstimulate, while forgetting about music, which can relax and soothe. Avoid music systems with brightly lit displays; these would appear startlingly bright in a softly lit bedroom. If the music-player is not beside your bed, choose a model with a remote control so that you can drift off to sleep without having to get up.

ROOM SCHEMES

best nest

The bedroom is the most intimate of places, and one that should make you feel secure and comfortable above any other. If you enjoy nesting, create a private boudoir complete with tactile throws, piles of cushions, and quilted coverings. Display some of your favourite clothes, photographs and keepsakes (if you have a lot of belongings, rotate your displays to avoid sensory overload). Indulge in feminine pink prints and mix them with solid pastel shades. In such a self-indulgent scheme, more is definitely more. Don't be censored by any notion that your room is not fashionable; decorate your space with whatever makes you feel good.

crisp and even

Crisp white bed linen creates a pure fresh look that doesn't date. It's also the easiest way to dress your bed, since duvet covers and sheets need not be in matching sets and can be washed at high temperatures. The lack of colour can give a rather monastic feel, however, and does nothing for pale complexions first thing in the morning. Combine plain white washable linens with throws and oversized reading pillows in rich or jewel-like colours. Extend the shots of colour to bedside lamps, rugs, artwork or a single wall.

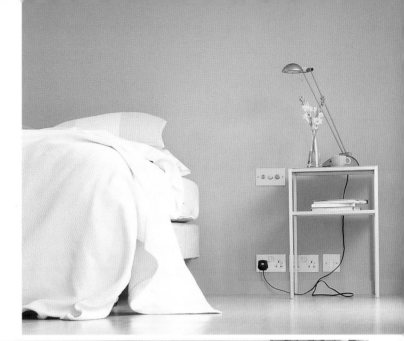

calm down

It is tempting to paint bedroom walls in advancing shades such as burnt orange, yellow or red to create instant warmth. While it is true that rich colour can make rooms feel intimate and cheerful, soft receding shades of blue and green are supremely calming, and will help you to take a deep breath at the end of the day. Paint walls or furniture – or display panels of fabric – in pure, 'clear-thinking' shades.

bathing
spaces

SPA-STYLE LUXURY

We ask a great deal of our bathrooms. Creating a functional and fresh 'wake-up' room that can be simply transformed into a relaxing, intimate haven is quite a challenge.

The next time you are having a leisurely soak in the bath, make a mental note of what things you would change about your existing bathroom if you could – and plan the layout of a new or redesigned bathing space accordingly.

Does the bathtub slope at the correct angle? Can you reach the taps easily? Is your towel on a heated rail nearby or will you have to get out of the bath to reach it? Is your sink big enough to wash your face without bumping your head on the taps? If not, a larger basin with neater taps could resolve this problem. Is the lavatory seat a bit too low? Contemporary wall-hung lavatories can be positioned at an optimum height (you can now even buy a lavatory with a heated seat!).

Rather than simply picking out what looks good, make a list of the concerns you have before visiting a showroom to find solutions.

A bathroom has a lifespan of at least ten years, so your choices should be able to stand the test of time. While appearance is not as important as comfort, an aesthetically pleasing and well-designed room will be a relaxing space to spend time in. When it comes to longevity and freshness, white remains the most satisfactory colour for bathroom suites; it can be brightened by coloured walls and accessories, or softened by ambient light.

With an abundance of designs to choose from, it can be difficult to decide on a style for your bathroom. Sleek lines and hard floor surfaces are the darlings of modern design, and contrast well with the architectural detailing found in period homes. Traditional slipper baths and

Victorian-style sinks are almost timeless in their appeal. But what really matters when choosing a style for your bathroom is that it harmonizes with the rest of your home. Ultra-contemporary designs are fantastic for those people who are minimalist by inclination, but if other rooms in your home are characterized by squashy chairs, freestanding cupboards and unruly houseplants, your bathroom should follow suit.

If you nurture fantasies of a bathroom that includes a large walk-in shower cubicle, double washbasins and a copious amount of storage space, you may need to tone these down for the average-sized bathroom.

A feeling of spaciousness is in itself a luxury, so, rather than squeezing too much into a small area, determine what is really important to you, and compromise on other things. For instance, a bidet may seem a necessity in a well-heeled bathroom, but how many times have you actually used one? (They are most useful in a downstairs cloakroom for washing dirty feet.) If you are desperate for a separate shower cubicle and don't tend to have many baths, consider putting in a short sitz bath to save space.

It pays to think laterally when you are trying to utilize all the available space in a small or awkwardly shaped room; for example, installing a sunken bath could create enough headroom for a bathing space in an attic with a sloping roof. Look for multifunctional items such as medicine cabinets with mirror doors and ladder radiators that heat the bathroom while drying and storing towels.

If, by making economies of space in other respects, you manage to find enough room for a favourite armchair or a double shower cubicle, everything will have been worth the effort.

LEFT *Bathrooms need to be planned in fine detail before building work commences, since there is generally little space for manoeuvre after plumbing and tiling. In this room, a generous sink unit allows plenty of space to display flowers or favourite toiletries, and a wall-mounted lavatory has been positioned at exactly the right height.*

BELOW *Fitting a bath beneath the sloping ceiling in this modest-sized bathroom cleverly maximizes the available space. If you plan to place a bath in an area of restricted height, make sure there is plenty of room to one side for towelling yourself dry after bathing.*

planning

If your bathroom needs a major overhaul, thorough planning in the early stages will avoid irritations later. Draw the room to scale on graph paper, noting the positions of the door, window, radiators and other fixed elements. Once you have chosen the components of the room, draw them separately so that you can experiment with various layouts. Consult a plumber about technicalities such as whether the water pressure is sufficient for a powerful shower.

Place items according to how you use your bathroom. If, for example, you enjoy long soaks, try to position the bath so that you have a view through the window or of a piece of art. Pair elements that are used in tandem; a bidet should be next to a lavatory, and a towel rail close to a bath or shower. If you are working to a budget, bear in mind that the position of the lavatory is the most expensive to change.

While most of us find fault with compact bathrooms, they do at least have the advantage that all the components of the room are close at hand. No matter how small your bathroom, allow ample space around each element for comfortable use. In particular, there should be plenty of space to dry yourself after a bath or shower, and enough leg-room in front of the lavatory.

Last but not least, don't forget the small but important details. Whether you would like a shelf to hold a radio or books or extra space around the bath for candles or a wine glass, take account of these elements from the start.

UPGRADING A BATHROOM

If a complete overhaul of your bathroom is impractical at the moment, there are several minor additions you can make to improve the one you have.

• **HEATED TOWEL RAIL** This looks sleeker and dries towels more quickly than a conventional radiator, as well as heating the room.

• **DIMMER SWITCH** A dimmer will allow you instantly to control and soften harsh, unflattering light.

• **NEW TOWELS** A set of plush bath towels introduces a touch of luxury.

• **FREESTANDING OR WALL-MOUNTED STORAGE UNIT** A cupboard may not seem to be a comfort essential, but the towels, toiletries and pampering goodies it holds are indispensable in the comfortable bathroom.

• **COTTON RUGS** Choose non-slip washable softies to cover up cold floors.

• **BATTERY-POWERED RADIO** This allows you to enjoy soothing music or your favourite drama series or soap while indulging in washing and pampering rituals.

baths

While few people would choose a bed without lying on it first, many buy baths without even sitting in them – but comfort should not be left to chance. If you are looking for a bath, go to the showroom with slip-on shoes and don't be reticent about asking to try before you buy. Once in the bath, stretch out, reach for the taps and check the position of the fittings. Baths, like people, come in all shapes and sizes. A standard rectangular bath uses water economically and lets the bather stretch out – and it may be the only option in a small room. But, while the dimensions of your bathroom are likely to limit your choice, there are several alternatives worth considering.

If you are petite or very tall, for example, look for baths with alternative proportions to standard-sized baths that will accommodate you more comfortably. Shorter-than-average and tapered baths are designed as space savers, but they are also ideal for shorter people who like to be able to touch the end of the bath when they stretch out. While corner baths take up more surface area, they are shorter than standard baths, which can leave wall space free for a sink or shower cubicle. They are a good choice for awkwardly shaped rooms and can visually correct long narrow spaces. Corner baths are ideal for sharing with your partner and for bathing children together. They do use a large quantity of water, however, and take longer to fill than regular baths.

Traditional slipper baths can be placed anywhere in the room to great effect. The elegant, high-shouldered design holds the bather in a slightly upright position – perfect for those who enjoy reading in the bath. Since the design tends to 'cuddle' the bather around the back and shoulders, think about an acrylic model that will feel warm against your skin.

Whirlpool baths contain a pump that mixes water with air to produce massaging jets while you bathe. Some also incorporate ambient lighting that can change the colours of the room to relax and energize you.

THIS PICTURE *Sunken baths are easy to step into and can be installed in bathrooms that have low or sloping ceilings, where the lack of headroom might otherwise be a problem.*

LEFT *Since they hold the bather in a slightly upright position, elegant, traditionally styled baths appeal to those who regard a good book and a good soak as the perfect partnership.*

FAR LEFT, ABOVE *This bathroom is spacious enough to accommodate a luxurious, centrally placed bath and an inviting armchair.*

FAR LEFT, BELOW *Round or corner baths are perfect for sharing, and often free up valuable wall space.*

RIGHT *This curvy bath has been decorated with simple white mosaic tiles. If you enjoy bathing à deux, centrally placed taps will ensure that neither of you gets the 'tap end'.*

showers

A hot, powerful shower can refresh and invigorate, while a tepid dribble serves as a daily irritant. If your shower falls into the second category, visualize a perfect shower before you visit the showroom. Do you enjoy being doused from overhead or would you rather use a directional spray to keep your hair and face dry? For all-over spray, some luxury units have multiple jets to massage you while you shower.

If you like to shower often, consider installing a dedicated cubicle. In tight spaces, look at downsizing the bath or removing a seldom-used item such as a bidet altogether.

LEFT *When splashing out on a new shower, make sure the cubicle is big enough. Standard-sized trays hardly leave room to pick up a dropped bar of soap, so it is well worth upgrading.*

BELOW LEFT *Doing away with shower trays, doors and curtains altogether is an increasingly popular option, but you will need to take planning advice from an expert to ensure that the room functions correctly.*

Give yourself some elbow room when choosing a shower cubicle. Standard-sized shower trays are a mere 80 cm (31 in) square, not leaving much room for picking up a dropped bar of soap. If space allows, choose a tray that is at least 90 cm (35 in) square. Larger cubicles also have room for integral seats, which can be extremely useful as you grow older or when you are feeling unwell.

When thinking about accessories, imagine yourself taking a shower. Is there a space to place soap and shampoo? Can you reach a warm towel easily when you've finished? Is there enough light to see what you're doing? Is there space to use a shower curtain without it sticking to you?

Not all showers are suitable for use with every boiler, and you will need to be familiar with your plumbing system before buying a shower. Whether you have a hot-water cylinder in the airing cupboard or a cold tank in the loft, the type of boiler and the strength and consistency of water pressure all have a bearing on the type of shower to choose.

CHOOSING A SHOWER

Sales staff can advise on suitable showers but it helps to review your priorities before you go shopping.

• **ELECTRIC SHOWER** An electric shower heats the water as it runs; the water won't run cold, however long you use it, but the flow may not be very strong. The higher the temperature is set, the weaker the flow.

• **POWER SHOWER** With its integral pump, a power shower has a greatly enhanced rate of flow. It offers easily adjustable pressure and temperature but uses up hot water more quickly than other showers.

• **MIXER SHOWER** This mixes existing hot and cold water and is likely to have a higher flow rate than an electric shower. It does not use up water as quickly as a power shower but cannot boost a weak flow. The flow rate and temperature of a mixer are usually affected when other appliances are being used.

• **THERMOSTATIC MIXER SHOWER** This incorporates a thermostat that senses changes in temperature and adjusts or cuts off the water flow accordingly.

• **BATH/SHOWER MIXER** In this arrangement, a hand-held showerhead uses the same water flow and taps as the bath; a diverter handle switches the flow from one to the other. This is a good option for washing your hair while in the bath.

BIG PICTURE AND INSET *Classic overhead showerheads are great for head-to-toe drenching. They are best combined with an adjustable, wall-mounted showerhead, which can be used on days when you don't want to wash your hair.*

LEFT *Make sure that drainage to your shower is adequate, particularly if you have selected a power shower that pumps high quantities of water. Nobody enjoys standing in a couple of inches of water while showering.*

towels & towel rails

Don't let a relaxing soak or an invigorating shower be spoilt by a towel that isn't to your taste. The longer and denser the cotton fibres or staples, the stronger, softer and more absorbent the towel will be. Towels made of long fibres wear better and produce less lint.

When applied to towels, the words 'Egyptian', 'Supima' and 'Brazilian' all indicate quality. Search for towels with a thread count of 180 or more (the thread count is the number of threads per square inch). Weight indicates quality. Softness does not. Some manufacturers add silicone-based additives that soften towelling. The resulting towels are less absorbent than untreated ones. Combed cotton is considered a top-quality fibre for towelling because only the best grades of cotton can be combed.

Standard bath towels are the perfect size for a good rub-down. They are also easier to dry and less bulky to store than larger towels. If you enjoy being swathed in an oversized towel, choose a bath sheet of about 90 cm (35 in) by 152 cm (60 in).

THIS PAGE *Good-quality towels are long-lasting and a pleasure to use. When shopping, look for weighty towels that are made of combed cotton and have a high thread count.*

Machine-wash towels in warm water with a mild detergent; tumble dry on the cotton setting and fold promptly. If you air-dry towels, shake them before hanging, and again when they are dry to fluff up the fabric loops. Avoid fabric softeners; they contain silicones that coat the cotton, stiffening towels and making them practically water-repellent. Good-quality towels should retain their soft texture for years without the use of fabric softener. As with bed linen, aim for three sets of towels for each family member and two more for visitors.

A towel rail is indispensable. Heated rails dry towels while occupying a minimal amount of space. They also heat the room, and keep towels warm once dry, ready for the next bath. Some rails can be hinged so that you can move them to the best spot for grabbing a warm towel after a shower. Modern designs can be positively sculptural, doubling as eye-catching wall art. If for any reason you can't fit a heated towel rail into your bathroom, use a traditional freestanding wooden version or hook a towel rack over the radiator.

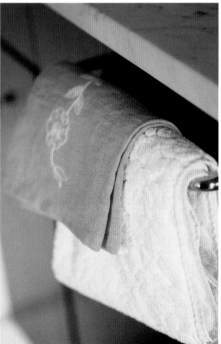

ABOVE *High-grade towels will last for years if they are properly laundered. Avoid fabric conditioners, which stiffen towels and affect their absorbency.*

LEFT AND FAR LEFT *Fit a heated towel rail if you can, since they help to heat the bathroom, provide warm towels after your bath or shower, and dry the towels after use. If a heated rail is not an option, place a freestanding rack or fit a rail close to the radiator.*

LEFT *Flooring need not be uniform throughout the entire bathroom. In this exceptionally narrow room, pale stone tiling is attractively combined with warm-toned wooden planks.*

FAR LEFT *Stone floors are elegant, practical and long-lasting, but chilly to walk on in bare feet. If your budget allows, invest in underfloor heating.*

flooring & lighting

Marble, slate, ceramic tiles and stone all make beautiful, durable bathroom floors, but, if you've ever walked barefoot on a stone floor first thing in the morning, you'll know how chilly they can be. For comfort, such floors should be installed with underfloor heating.

Wood and laminate floors feel warmer underfoot. They also have natural 'give', making them easier on feet and legs. Look for newer versions that will not warp or buckle, regardless of the amount of moisture in the room. Rubber is available in tile or sheet form, and in a huge range of colours and textures; as well as being quiet, waterproof and non-slip, rubber floors feel warm and sensual underfoot. Vinyl and linoleum are also appealing options. Durable, warm and gentle on the feet, such floors are easy to maintain. They come in many colours and designs, including stone- and tile-effect finishes.

Carpet is warm, comfortable and quiet, but can get soggy in a bathroom. Washable throw rugs (with non-slip backing) are a better solution.

Successful bathroom lighting requires a mix of directed light for tasks such as applying make-up and shaving and ambient light for relaxing and soaking in the tub. For task lighting, aim for a balance between harsh light and a dim but flattering glow. Avoid a single light in the centre of the ceiling, since this will cast shadows and be too bright for early morning. Several spotlights on a dimmer switch will be much more satisfactory. Downlighting is good for bathrooms, and since the room layout will remain static, you can aim light accurately. Place small recessed halogen spots wherever they are needed.

For ambient light, uplighters wash the walls with soft colour. Light in bathrooms needn't be very strong. Fit the main lights with a dimmer switch so that you can fine-tune at will, since white suites and tiles reflect the light. Dress bathroom windows minimally to maximize natural light. Use frosted, coloured or etched glass for privacy.

ABOVE AND TOP *Task lighting for shaving or applying make-up should be effective but kind. It is preferable not to have to stare at your face in an unflatteringly harsh light.*

LEFT *Natural light sources are often overlooked in bathrooms. Here, a skylight creates a beautiful pool of light in a simple but comfortably furnished space.*

FINISHES

artwork Rather than being limited to gazing at plain white tiling while you soak in the tub, adorn the bathroom walls as you would any other room in your home. If damage from excessive moisture is a concern, restrict your choice to inexpensive prints, decorative platters or a beautiful gilt mirror.

storage A soak in the bath will not be relaxing if you are surrounded by clutter, no matter how many scented oils or candles you use. Good storage is a necessity in a bathroom. If space is tight, look for hanging baskets, containers to fit under the sink or tall skinny storage units that take up the minimum of floor space. If you have more room to play with, invest in a generous towel cupboard.

indulgences Make space in a bathroom for the activities you enjoy there. Install a shelf for items such as a radio in a spot that will not receive any accidental splashes. Fit a bookcase or a few shelves, and fill them with books and magazines that you enjoy revisiting. If your bath doesn't incorporate a ledge wide enough to support a glass of wine or a teacup, keep a small stool or table in the room that can be pulled up close to the bath when needed.

chairs

A bathroom chair is a place where you can sit and chat to someone taking a bath or supervise children while they are in the water. You can also use it while waiting for the bathtub to fill or to dry off after bathing. Towelling-covered seat pads are both comfortable and practical for bathrooms, wicker chairs give a slightly nautical feel, while Lloyd Loom seats evoke English country gardens.

bath rack

A bath rack may seem rather old-fashioned, but don't discount an excellent idea just because it has been around for a while. Bath racks are perfect for holding books, candles and pampering goodies. Classic wire racks look attractive, but alternatives with smaller gaps between the slats are more useful.

candles

Candles are flattering, atmospheric and mood-enhancing, and can transform the starkest white bathroom into a relaxing haven. Buy inexpensive nightlights in bulk and use them liberally. Keep a good supply of them in a glass jar or basket in your bathroom.

practical priority

A well-thought-out, superbly functional bathroom will wash away worries. Choose crisp white tiles and large towels to match. If planning from scratch, think about the number of toiletries you use regularly, and keep them close to hand on built-in shelves around the bath or in the shower. If you share your bathroom with someone else, invest in a double sink so that you won't be fighting to clean your teeth. Decorate the room simply and neutrally to let the clean lines and smooth curves of your bath and basin speak for themselves.

blooming colour

Bright white bathrooms may wake you up in the early morning – but they are just too dazzling for a leisurely evening soak in the tub. Nobody is suggesting a return to avocado suites, but a little wall colour goes a long way. Choose a calm contemplative shade of blue or green or rich advancing tones of red or terracotta to put you in the mood. (Don't forget to light lots of candles and have a soothing drink close at hand.)

anything goes

Bathroom suites may be immovable, but otherwise unstructured bathing areas accommodate both changing needs and well-loved furniture with ease. They offer places to set down a book or a glass of wine and give the bathroom a relaxed, individual, lived-in feel. Build up an eclectic collection of objects to create a quirky room that will put a smile on your face in the morning. Look for small tables or trolleys that will squeeze between fixed elements to hold toiletries, books and towels.

outdoor spaces

GARDEN COMFORTS

Most of us have embraced the contemporary idea of using the garden (if we have one) as an extension of our home – an outdoor 'room' for dining and relaxing. Our expectations of comfort in these newly rediscovered spaces, though, are often far lower than what we aspire to indoors. There is no reason to suffer an uncomfortable chair just because it stands on the patio instead of in the living room. Outdoor lighting systems and heaters mean that we don't need to sit in the dark or endure the evening chill. Think of the activities you like doing in your garden and the times of day when you most enjoy being there, and furnish it accordingly.

As long as the weather is mild, there is no reason to abandon your garden after the sun has gone down. Artificial light can turn a dark patio into a 'dining room' and add a sculptural quality to shrubs or garden ornaments. Low-voltage spotlights on spikes can be sunk into the ground along with a transformer relatively easily. Circuits for larger gardens are linked to a home's mains voltage system and should be installed by a qualified technician. A master switch placed inside the house can operate most outdoor light systems.

If the thought of installing a lighting system daunts you, a charming effect can be achieved by stringing up a row of outdoor fairy lights; the twinkling strands can be used to mark out a dining or seating area. Candlelight is instant and cheap, and easiest of all. Place nightlights in jars or lanterns and scatter them around the garden, or use them to illuminate a path or stairway. Citronella-scented candles on sticks can be pushed into the ground to ward off bugs.

Parasols and sun umbrellas provide shade and sun protection on hot days, and many garden tables have a central hole that you can slot them into. Choose a large umbrella to avoid frequent repositioning as the sun moves around. Awnings can be made very simply from a piece of canvas with eyelets in each corner. Tie them with rope to poles, trees or the side of the house. Again, make sure they are a good size. Tall plants can create beautiful homegrown shade and privacy. Train flowering climbers over trellis or branch structures, or plant long tall Sallies such as delphiniums and hollyhocks.

Place a garden table close to the house so that you are near the kitchen if you forget items needed for alfresco meals. When entertaining friends, try not to make things too complicated. Prepare simple food that doesn't mind waiting a little before it is eaten. Round or oval serving bowls take up less space on the table, and can be carried to the table easily. Invest in large trays so that you don't have to make frequent trips to the kitchen. Keep a couple of cake covers handy to prevent bugs and flies from trying to share your meal. If you are a night owl, outdoor heaters take the chill out of the air, allowing you to stay in your garden for longer.

Whether you live in a city apartment, a rural retreat or a suburban semi, let your garden transport you to wherever you'd really like to be. Create a cottage garden with a rustic bench, floral printed cushions and traditional border planting or a calming Zen space with smooth pebbles, bamboos and simple wooden furniture – or evoke memories of a seaside holiday with shells, grasses and jaunty deck chairs.

tables & chairs

Outdoor furniture should complement a garden's style and level of formality – but, above all, it should feel as good as it looks. Wirework chairs, for example, may add romance to a rose garden but can become too hot to sit on in midday sun. Pieces can be freestanding or built-in, and materials include wood, stone, iron, wirework, rattan, wickerwork and plastic.

Wood does not get too hot or cold, and mostly weathers well, making it an excellent option for freestanding furniture. Rot-resistant teak does not have to be sealed, stained or finished, and gradually weathers to an attractive silver-grey. Cedar is much lighter than teak and ages gracefully; the

wood lies flat and stays straight. Pine does not last long, however; most pine tables and chairs will warp, splinter and rot when left outside, unless treated with preservatives.

Rattan and wickerwork look good both indoors or out, and woven chairs have a pleasing 'give' as you sit in them. These materials do not become too hot or cold, although wickerwork can snap, creating sharp edges; they must be stored inside at night and in winter.

Built-in seating is most easily introduced when you are planning a garden. Permanent furniture can make gardens look less cluttered and give an illusion of space. Simple

LEFT *If you are unsure what material to choose, put together an eclectic collection like this one, which mixes plastic, wood and wirework. Although it can get uncomfortably hot in the sun, plastic furniture is inexpensive, lightweight and often stackable.*

ABOVE *Stone makes beautiful and sturdy tabletops that won't rot, warp or rust, but it is very heavy, making the furniture hard to move.*

ABOVE LEFT *A couple of fat cushions add comfort to a simple metal bench.*

MAKING THE MOST OF GARDEN FURNITURE

Before buying furniture, measure your garden to find out what will fit where conveniently. A modest table with four chairs occupies about 2.5 square metres (25 square feet). If space is tight, choose folding tables and chairs.

• SET UP FURNITURE CLOSE TO HOME Proximity to the kitchen makes alfresco dining much easier than it would otherwise be.

• PLACE DINING TABLES IN PARTIAL SHADE Dappled sunlight is best; if there is no natural shade, add simple awnings, fabric knotted to a pole or an oversized parasol.

• AVOID STANDING WATER It will rot or rust tabletops – so create a slight tilt when positioning a table, or choose a design with slats or drainage holes.

• SOAK UP THE SUN Place loungers in a central position so that you won't have to move them repeatedly to follow the sun.

• SEE WHO'S COMING When placing chairs in hidden corners, arrange them so that they face the direction of the house.

ABOVE *Hammocks are cosy and cosseting, and have no hard edges, but they require plenty of space between tying posts. If you haven't got trees or posts in the correct position, the alternative is a large 'freestanding' hammock.*

wood or stone pieces allow the focus to remain on the garden itself, while more elaborate designs can add a sculptural quality. Built-in furniture tends to be more expensive than freestanding pieces, and the obvious disadvantage is its permanence; tables and chairs need to be carefully positioned. Pay particular attention to the gap between chairs and table. If it is too small, you will have trouble sitting down or getting up; if it is too large, you will be stretching to reach your food.

A long wooden bench can seat several people – and with the addition of a cushion becomes a lounger for just one. Make sure that deck chairs and recliners can be set up and adjusted easily. Sit in the recliner and check that the armrests are at the right height. Are they adjustable? Is the recliner long enough? Recliners and sun loungers with wheels make for 1950s-style glamour and easy repositioning. Choose cushion covers in pale cotton canvas. Pale tones reflect heat and stay cooler than dark or bright shades.

porches, conservatories & summerhouses

Spaces that are neither inside nor out have universal appeal. In hot climates, porches are wrapped around homes to give shady respite from the heat. In cool climates, conservatories maximize the available sunlight and warmth. Summerhouses act as dens and treehouses for adults. If connected to electricity and water supplies, they can even provide workplaces or guest annexes.

OPPOSITE *Even if it is positioned only a short distance from the house, a summerhouse offers a respite from life's daily hurly-burly.*

LEFT *A simple timber structure that has been decked out with inviting furniture and sparkling lights offers an enchanting outdoor room.*

BELOW *Conservatories serve to maximize sunlight and warmth in cooler climates. If you want to use the space all year round, fit blinds to provide shade from the sun and install heating for chillier months.*

Before allowing brochures and showroom models to seduce you, consider how and when you will use your indoor-outdoor room. For winter use, you may need heating, cavity-wall insulation and double-glazing. Structures with large areas of glass on three sides will give several viewpoints. (The room will also be sunnier and warmer for more of the day.) The sound of rain falling on a plastic roof can be deafening, so choose glass, wood or roof tiles if you like sitting in the rain.

North-facing rooms offer even light with no direct sunlight, while a south-facing elevation receives maximum sun. For sun without excessive heat or glare, west- or east-facing rooms are ideal. If you plan to dine regularly in the indoor-outdoor space, try to site it close to the kitchen – or you'll have to traipse though the house with hot food. If you plan to use the space after dark, you will need to install power points for lighting. Avoid single centrally placed fittings, which cast an unflattering light. Uplighters placed on solid walls will provide ambience, while table and standard lamps fitted with tungsten bulbs will create pools of warm light.

FINISHES

lighting   You can use lighting to transform your garden into an outdoor sitting area after dark. Candlelight is supremely simple and inexpensive – but protect the lighted wick with a glass jar or a hurricane lamp. Outdoor fairy lights are simple to string up and create a magical atmosphere. Electric lights on spikes can be pushed into the ground to illuminate paths and highlight sculptures and trees.

water   Running water is well known for its meditative properties. If you have enough space, consider installing a pond in your garden; if not, a small rippling water feature will have a similar calming effect.

sculpture

Sculpture need not be highbrow nor as simple as a pair of stone cherubs from the local garden centre. Either create your own artwork with found objects or commission a piece for a specific area of your garden. Sculpture will provide points of interest, particularly in winter, when foliage and flowers are sparse

window boxes

No matter how little outdoor space you have, you can influence it for the better. Window boxes are accessible to everyone, and can be used to grow cheerful blooms, beautifully scented plants or aromatic herbs. If your garden centre doesn't have any interesting planters, customize one with a coat of paint – or try making your own.

GARDEN SCHEMES

urban cool

Outdoor spaces can be transformed into cool urban-style sitting rooms, both during the day and at night. For example, you can lay a decking floor and fit outdoor lighting. Furnish the room simply with wicker or canvas armchairs and add a sprinkling of potted plants, herbs or shrubs.

eastern idyll

Japanese gardens promote a sense of order, calm and tranquillity. Mimic their simple style by planting tall grasses and bamboos that will rustle mesmerically in the breeze. Place rustic wooden furniture in a shady spot for meditation and complete relaxation, and add cushions to make it more comfortable.

country comfort

Rambling roses and white garden furniture evoke an irresistible country style, whether you live in a rural or an urban location. Choose wicker or metalwork chairs and pad them with plenty of cushions for comfort; the more floral prints and candy stripes the better.

sources

Elements of a comfortable home can be found at all sorts of retail outlets. The following selection of shops stock good-quality home and garden furnishings, and will provide a starting point in your quest for comfort.

Anna French
343 Kings Road
London SW3 5ES
020 7351 1126
www.annafrench.co.uk
Fabrics, wallpapers and accessories.

Armitage Shanks
Armitage
Rugeley
Staffordshire WS15 4BT
01543 490253
www.armitage-shanks.co.uk
Bathroom fixtures.

Bulthaup
37 Wigmore Street
London W1U 1PN
020 7495 3663 for stockists
www.bulthaup.com
Contemporary kitchen furniture.

Christy
www.christy-towels.com
08457 585252
Towels, bed linen and accessories.

The Conran Shop
Michelin House
81 Fulham Road
London SW3 6RD
020 7589 7401
www.conran.co.uk
Contemporary furniture, storage and accessories.

C.P. Hart
213 Newnham Terrace
Hercules Road
London SE1 7DR
020 7902 1000
www.cphart.co.uk
Modern bathrooms.

Crocus
www.crocus.co.uk
0870 787 1413
Online garden centre selling plants and tools.

Designers Guild
267–71 & 275–77 King's Road
London SW3 5EN
020 7351 5775 for store
020 7243 7300 for stockists and mail order
www.designersguild.com
Contemporary paint colours; inspiring fabrics and wallpapers.

Feather & Black
www.featherandblack.com
stockists: 01243 380 600
Bedding and bed linen.

The Floor Warming Company
2 School Parade
High Street, Harefield
Middlesex UB9 6BT
01895 825288
www.floorwarmingcompany.co.uk
Electric underfloor heating systems.

Forbes & Lomax
205a St John's Hill
London SW11 1TH
020 7738 0202
www.forbesandlomax.co.uk
Switches, sockets and dimmers in perspex, frosted acrylic and metals.

General Trading Company
2 Symons Street
London SW3 2TJ
020 7730 0411
www.generaltrading.co.uk
Contemporary furniture and accessories.

The Hardwood Flooring Company
146–52 West End Lane
London NW6 1SD
020 7328 8481
www.hardwoodflooringcompany.com
Extensive choice of timber flooring.

Habitat
www.habitat.net
for a store near you
Furniture for indoors and outdoors.

Heal's
196 Tottenham Court Road
London W1T 7LQ
020 7636 1666
www.heals.co.uk
Furniture, accessories and storage.

The Holding Company
241–45 King's Road
London SW3 5EL
020 7352 1600
020 8445 2888 mail order
www.theholdingcompany.co.uk
Storage with style.

The Home Office
TempleCo Ten
Stonestile Barn
Harthill, Charing
Kent TN27 0HW
01233 712710
Self-contained work spaces and garden rooms.

Ikea
www.ikea.com
for a store near you
Kitchen units, furniture and storage.

John Cullen Lighting
585 Kings Road
London SW6 2EH
020 7371 5400
www.johncullenlighting.co.uk
A wide range of discreet fittings; lighting design service.

John Lewis
www.johnlewis.com
for a store near you
Department stores with everything for the home.

Judy Greene's Garden Store
11 Flask Walk
London NW3 1HJ
020 7435 3832
Unusual range of garden furniture and accessories.

Lloyd Christie
103 Lancaster Road
London W11 1QN
020 7243 6466
Luxurious summerhouses and modern urban-garden accessories.

Nu-Heat
Heathpark Industrial Estate
Honiton
Devon EX14 1SD
01404 549770
www.nu-heat.co.uk
Water-based underfloor heating systems.

SKK Lighting
34 Lexington Street
London W1F OLH
020 7434 4095
www.skk.net
Modern lighting specialists.

Smeg
08708 243781 for stockists and information.
www.smeguk.com
Stainless-steel kitchen appliances.

Sofa Workshop
01443 238 699
www.sofaworkshop.com
Sofas and sofa beds.

Sottini
The Bathroom Works
National Avenue
Kingston upon Hull
HU5 4HS
01482 449513
www.sottini.co.uk
Bathroom fixtures.

Stone Age
Unit 3, Parsons Green Depot
Parsons Green Lane
London SW6 4HH
020 7384 9090
www.stone-age.co.uk
Limestone and sandstone flooring and worktops made to order.

The White Company
0870 900 9555
www.thewhitecompany.com
for a store near you
Linens, furniture and accessories for bedrooms, bathrooms and dining rooms.

picture credits

key: ph= photographer, a=above, b=below, r=right, l=left, c=centre.

Page 1 ph Polly Wreford; 2 ph Polly Wreford/the Sawmills Studios; 3 ph Tom Leighton; 4-5 ph Debi Treloar/Debi Treloar's family home in north-west London; 5 both ph Debi Treloar; 6 ph Christopher Drake/William Yeoward & Colin Orchard's home in London; 7bl ph Christopher Drake/Ali Sharland's house in Gloucestershire; 7ar ph Christopher Drake/Enrica Stabile's house in Le Thor, Provence; 8l ph Polly Wreford/Kathy Moskal's apartment in New York designed by Ken Foreman; 8-9 ph Polly Wreford/Ros Fairman's house in London; 9 ph Polly Wreford/Carol Reid's apartment in Paris; 10 ph Catherine Gratwicke/Francesca Mills' house in London, 1970s scarf cushions from Maisonette; 11l ph Christopher Drake/an apartment in Milan designed by Daniela Micol Wajskol, interior designer; 11r Morag Myerscough's house in Clerkenwell, London, her house gallery/shop, photograph by Richard Learoyd; 12l ph Andrew Wood/Michael Asplund's apartment in Stockholm, Sweden; 12-13 ph Debi Treloar/Susan Cropper's family home in London, www.63hlg.com; 13a ph Alan Williams; 13b ph Chris Everard/designed by Mullman Seidman Architects; 14l ph Chris Tubbs/Phil Lapworth's treehouse near Bath; 14r ph Christopher Drake; 15 ph Chris Tubbs/Nickerson-Wakefield House in upstate New York/anderson architects; 16-17 ph Jan Baldwin/interior designer Didier Gomez's apartment in Paris; 17 ph Jan Baldwin/Christopher Leach's apartment in London; 18 ph Tom Leighton; 19l ph Catherine Gratwicke; 19c ph Jan Baldwin/Emma Wilson's house in London; 19r ph Christopher Drake/Josephine Ryan's house in London; 20 ph Polly Wreford; 21a ph Nicki Dowey/pillows from Feather & Black, armchair from Sofa Workshop; 21b ph Nicki Dowey/armchair from Sofa Workshop; 22r ph Christopher Drake/Enrica Stabile's house in Milan; 22l ph James Merrell; 23 ph Chris Everard/an apartment in Milan designed by Daniela Micol Wajskol, interior designer; 24l ph Tom Leighton; 24-25 ph Debi Treloar/Jill Henry & Jon Pellicoro's family home in New York, artwork by Jon Pellicoro; 25 ph Chris Everard/designed by Mullman Seidman Architects; 26-27 ph Chris Everard/Sig.ra Venturini's apartment in Milan; 27a&bl ph Jan Baldwin; 25br ph Jan Baldwin/Clare Mosley's house in London; 28l ph Jan Baldwin/Mona Nerenberg and Lisa Bynon's house in Sag Harbor; 28r ph Andrew Wood/Christer Wallensteen's apartment in Stockholm, Sweden; 29 ph Jan Baldwin/interior designer Didier Gomez's apartment in Paris; 30-31 ph Debi Treloar/designer Susanne Rutzou's home in Copenhagen; 31a ph Jan Baldwin/Laurence & Yves Sabourets' house in Brittany; 31b ph Polly Wreford/Kathy Moskal's apartment in New York designed by Ken Foreman; 32 ph Polly Wreford/Courtney Brennan's apartment in New York designed by Ken Foreman; 33al ph Ray Main; 33ar ph Chris Everard; 33b ph Ray Main/a house in East Hampton, interior by Vicente Wolf; 34l ph James Merrell; 34r ph Chris Everard/Charles Bateson's house in London; 35 both ph Ray Main; 36al ph Sandra Lane/cushions from Jane Sacchi; 36ar ph Sandra Lane/cushions by Sasha Gibb; 36c ph Sandra Lane/quilt, cushion and throw from Graham & Green; 36b ph Debi Treloar; 37a ph Catherine Gratwicke/Laura Stoddart's apartment in London; 37cl ph Sandra Lane/cushions and throw by Karen Nicol; 37c ph Sandra Lane/throw from Muskett & Mazzullo; 37cr ph Sandra Lane/Laurent Bayard's home in London, throw made by Laurent Bayard; 37bl ph Chris Tubbs; 37br ph Christopher Drake; 38a ph James Merrell/Sue and Andy A'Court's apartment in Blackheath, London; 38cl ph Catherine Gratwicke/Francesca Mills' house in London, cushions from After Noah; 38r ph Alan Williams/Lindsay Taylor's apartment in Glasgow; 38b & 39bl ph Debi Treloar/a family home in London; 39al ph Polly Eltes/curtain design by Sian and Annie Colley; 39ar ph

Polly Eltes/designed by Carden Cunietti; 39c ph Catherine Gratwicke/Elena Colombo's apartment in New York; 39br ph Alan Williams/Stanley & Nancy Grossman's apartment in New York designed by Jennifer Post Design; 40 ph Debi Treloar/Susan Cropper's family home in London, www.63hlg.com; 41a ph Christopher Drake/Fay & Roger Oates' house in Ledbury; 41b ph Alan Williams/the architect Voon Wong's own apartment in London; 42a ph Polly Wreford/Mary Foley's house in London; 42bl ph Jan Baldwin/Emma Wilson's house in London; 42br ph Polly Wreford/Ann Shore's former home in London; 43a ph Christopher Drake/William Yeoward & Colin Orchard's home in London; 43b ph Christopher Drake/Fay & Roger Oates' house in Ledbury; 44-45 ph Jan Baldwin/the Meiré family home, designed by Marc Meiré; 45 ph Jan Baldwin; 46 ph Tom Leighton/Fay & Roger Oates' house in Ledbury; 47l ph Tom Leighton; 47c ph James Merrell/Robyn and Simon Carnachan's house in Auckland; 47r ph Jan Baldwin/Constanze von Unruh's house in London; 48 ph Chris Everard/architect Jonathan Clark's home in London; 49l ph Simon Upton; 49r ph Chris Everard/Suze Orman's apartment in New York designed by Mullman Seidman Architects; 50l ph Chris Everard/Jo Warman, Interior Concepts; 50r ph James Merrell/Linda Parham and David Slobham's apartment in Sydney designed by architect Stephen Varady; 51l ph Alan Williams/Alannah Weston's house in London designed by Stickland Coombe Architecture; 51r ph Andrew Wood/Jamie Falla and Lynn Graham's house in London; 51b ph Chris Everard/designer Karim Rashid's own apartment in New York; 52 ph Debi Treloar/Nicky Phillips' apartment in London; 53 main ph Jan Baldwin/the owner of Tessuti, Catherine Vindevogel-Debal's house in Kortrijk, Belgium, kitchen designed by Filip Van Bever; 53 inset ph James Merrell/Christine Walsh and Ian Bartlett's house in London deigned by Jack Ingham of Bookworks; 54l ph Tom Leighton; 54-55 ph Alan Williams/Alannah Weston's house in London designed by Stickland Coombe Architecture; 55b ph James Merrell; 55a ph Chris Everard/Vicson Guevara's apartment in New York designed by Yves-Claude Design; 55b ph Christopher Drake/Ali Sharland's house in Gloucestershire; 56a ph Chris Everard/Hudson Street Loft, designed by Moneo Brock Studio; 56-57 ph Andrew Wood/the home of Gwen Aldridge and Bruce McLucas; 58a ph Chris Everard/designed by Mullman Seidman Architects; 58b ph Andrew Wood; 59a ph Chris Everard/Hudson Street Loft, designed by Moneo Brock Studio; 59b ph Chris Everard/John Barman's Park Avenue apartment; 60b ph James Merrell; 60a Polly Wreford/the Sawmills Studio; 61al&bl ph James Merrell; 61ar ph Chris Everard; 61br ph Chris Everard; 62 ph Chris Everard/designed by Mullman Seidman Architects; 63l ph Chris Everard/Vicson Guevara's apartment in New York designed by Yves-Claude Design; 63r ph Jan Baldwin/Emma Wilson's house in London; 64l ph Chris Everard/Nadav Kander & Nicole Verity's house; 64r ph Chris Everard/Charles Bateson's house in London; 65l ph Chris Everard/John Barman's Park Avenue apartment; 65r ph Henry Bourne; 66-67 ph Chris Everard/designed by Mullman Seidman Architects; 67l ph Ray Main/Jonathan Reed's apartment in London, lighting designed by Sally Storey, design director of John Cullen Lighting; 67r ph Jan Baldwin/Peter & Nicole Dawes' apartment, designed by Mullman Seidman Architects; 68l ph James Merrell; 68r ph Andrew Wood/Jamie Falla and Lynn Graham's house in London; 69l ph James Merrell; 69c ph Andrew Wood; 69r ph Chris Everard/Vicson Guevara's apartment in New York designed by Yves-Claude Design; 70a ph Chris Tubbs; 70cl ph Andrew Wood; 70cr ph Chris Everard; 70bl ph Chris Everard/Kampfner's house in London designed by Ash Sakula Architects; 70bc ph Debi Treloar; 70br ph Debi Treloar/owner's of Maisonette, Martin Barrell & Amanda Sellers' home in London; 71al ph Christopher Drake/a house designed by artist Angela A'Court; 71ac ph Alan Williams/Louise Robbins' house in north-west Herefordshire; 71ar ph Christopher Drake/Lincoln Cato's house in Brighton; 71c both ph Jan Baldwin; 71bl ph Christopher Drake; 72a ph Simon Upton; 72c ph Jan Baldwin/Clare Mosley's house in London; 72bl ph Alan

Williams/Louise Robbins' house in north-west Herefordshire; **72bc** *ph* James Merrell; **72br** *ph* Debi Treloar/Debi Treloar's home in London; **73al** *ph* James Merrell/Janick and Hubert Schoumacher-Vilfroy's house in Normandy; **73ac** *ph* James Merrell; **73ar** *ph* Ray Main/Nello Renault's loft in Paris; **72cl&cr** *ph* Jan Baldwin; **72c** *ph* Debi Treloar; **73b** *ph* Tom Leighton; **74** *ph* Christopher Drake/Monique Davidson's family home in Normandy; **75a** *ph* Debi Treloar/Paul Balland and Jane Wadham of jwflowers.com's family home in London; **75r** *ph* Christopher Drake/a house in Salisbury designed by Helen Ellery of The Plot London; **76 inset** *ph* Jan Baldwin/interior designer Didier Gomez's apartment in Paris; **76 main** *ph* Henry Bourne; **77al** *ph* Jan Baldwin/architect Joseph Dirand's apartment in Paris; **77bl** *ph* Jan Baldwin/Mark Smith's home in the Cotswolds; **77r** *ph* Debi Treloar/Robert Elms and Christina Wilson's family home in London; **78–79** *ph* Debi Treloar/Susan Cropper's family home in London, www.63hlg.com; **79** *ph* Dan Duchars; **80** *ph* Henry Bourne; **81l** *ph* Debi Treloar/Robert Elms and Christina Wilson's family home in London; **81c** *ph* Jan Baldwin; **81r** *ph* Debi Treloar/architect Simon Colebrook's home in London; **82l** *ph* Dan Duchars; **82–83** *ph* Christopher Drake/designed by McLean Quinlan Architects; **84** *ph* Polly Wreford/Ros Fairman's house in London; **85l** *ph* Polly Wreford/Louise Jackson's house in London; **85r** *ph* Dan Duchars; **86l** *ph* Sandra Lane/vintage cushion from Cath Kidston, mattress made by Pat Giddens; **86–87 & 87r** *ph* Nicki Dowey/mattress from John Lewis, featherbed topper from The White Company, bed frame from Habitat; **88l** *ph* Jan Baldwin/Olivia Douglas & David DiDomenico's apartment in New York, designed by CR Studio Architects, PC; **88r** *ph* Chris Everard/Programmable House in London, designed by d–squared; **89** *ph* Jan Baldwin/designer Chester Jones' house in London; **90l** *ph* Nicki Dowey/duvet from Feather & Black; **90–91** *ph* Nicki Dowey/pink quilt from Anna French, duvets from Feather & Black; **91** *ph* Jan Baldwin/Angela and David Coxon's family home in Kent; **92** *ph* Jan Baldwin/David Gill's house in London; **93l** *ph* Dan Duchars; **93r** *ph* Nicki Dowey/mattress from John Lewis, pillows from Feather & Black; **94** *ph* Tom Leighton/Fay & Roger Oates' house in Ledbury; **95l&br** *ph* Polly Wreford/Mary Foley's house in Connecticut; **95ar** *ph* Henry Bourne; **96 both** *ph* Debi Treloar/Cristine Tholstrup Hermansen and Helge Drenck's house in Copenhagen; **97l** *ph* Jan Baldwin; **97r** *ph* Jan Baldwin/Sophie Eadie's family home in London; **98** *ph* Alan Williams/Louise Robbins' house in north-west Herefordshire; **99a** *ph* Simon Upton; **99b** *ph* Polly Wreford; **100a** *ph* Andrew Wood/Guido Palau's house in north London, designed by Azman Owens Architects; **100cl** *ph* Tom Leighton, **100cr** *ph* James Merrell; **100bl** *ph* Jan Baldwin/the Fitzwilliam-Lay's family home, interior design by Henri Fitzwilliam-Lay and Totem Design; **100br** *ph* Jan Baldwin/the owner of Tessuti, Catherine Vindevogel-Debal's house in Kortrijk, Belgium; **101al & 101ar** *ph* Jan Baldwin; **101cl** *ph* Ray Main/Robert Callender & Elizabeth Ogilvie's studio in Fife designed by John C Hope Architects; **101r & 101b** *ph* James Merrell; **102a** *ph* Polly Wreford/Kimberley Watson's house in London; **102b** *ph* Christopher Drake/Nordic Style Bedroom; **103a** *ph* Alan Williams/Alannah Weston's house in London designed by Stickland Coombe Architecture; **103b** *ph* Jan Baldwin/Wendy Jansen and Chris Van Eldik, owners of J.O.B. Interieur's house in Wijk bij Duurstede, The Netherlands; **104** *ph* Polly Wreford/Ros Fairman's house in London; **105a** *ph* Tom Leighton; **105b** *ph* Simon Upton; **106–107** Polly Wreford/Ros Fairman's house in London; **107** *ph* Henry Bourne; **108** *ph* Polly Wreford; **109l&cl** *ph* Polly Wreford/Kimberley Watson's house in London; **109cr** *ph* Henry Bourne; **109r** *ph* Dan Duchars/Susan Cropper's family home in London, www.63hlg.com; **110l** *ph* Chris Everard/the Sugarman–Behun house on Long Island; **110r** *ph* Chris Everard/Sig.ra Venturini's apartment in Milan; **111 main** *ph* Alan Williams/Richard Oyarzarbal's apartment in London designed by Urban Research Laboratory; **111 inset** *ph* Alan Williams/Alannah Weston's house in London designed by Stickland Coombe Architecture; **112al** *ph* Chris Everard/Philippa Rose's house in London designed by Caroline Paterson/

Victoria Fairfax of Paterson Gornall Interiors, together with Clive Butcher Designs; **112bl** *ph* Chris Everard/an apartment in Paris designed by Bruno Tanquerel; **112r** *ph* Catherine Gratwicke/the brownstone in New York of Bonnie Young, director of global sourcing and inspiration at Donna Karan International; **113a** *ph* Chris Everard/John Eldridge's loft apartment in London designed by Seth Stein; **113b** *ph* Christopher Drake/a house designed by artist Angela A'Court; **114l** *ph* Jan Baldwin/a house in New York designed by Brendan Coburn and Joseph Smith from Coburn Architecture; **114r** James Morris/a loft apartment in London designed by Simon Conder Associates **115 main** *ph* Chris Everard/Suze Orman's apartment in New York designed by Mullman Seidman Architects; **115 insets** *ph* Chris Everard; **116** *ph* Andrew Wood; **117l** *ph* Chris Everard; **117c** *ph* Jan Baldwin; **117r** Nicki Dowey/towels from Christy; **118l** *ph* James Merrell/François Gilles & Dominique Lubar, IPL Interiors; **118r** *ph* Chris Everard/Simon Brignall & Christina Rosetti's loft apartment in London designed by David Mikhail Architects; **118-19** *ph* Debi Treloar/Kristiina Ratia and Jeff Gocke's family home in Norwalk, Connecticut; **119a** *ph* Ray Main/Andrea Luria and Zachary Feuer's house in Los Angeles designed by Studio Works, Robert Mangurian and Mary-Ann Ray; **119b** *ph* Ray Main/a house in Pennsylvania designed by Jeffrey Bilhuber; **120a** *ph* Debi Treloar/author, stylist and owner of Caravan (shop) Emily Chalmers and director Chris Richmond's home in London; **120cl** *ph* Debi Treloar; **120cr** *ph* Tom Leighton; **120b** *ph* Debi Treloar/Robert Elms and Christina Wilson's family home in London; **121al** *ph* Debi Treloar/author, stylist and owner of Caravan (shop) Emily Chalmers and director Chris Richmond's home in London; **121ar** *ph* Christopher Drake/Eva Johnson's house in Suffolk, interiors designed by Eva Johnson; **121c** *ph* Henry Bourne; **121bl** *ph* Chris Everard; **121br** David Brittain; **122** *ph* Jan Baldwin/art dealer Gul Coskun's apartment in London; **123l** *ph* Chris Everard/an apartment in Milan designed by Daniela Micol Wajskol, interior designer; **123r both** *ph* Alan Williams/Gail & Barry Stephens' house in London; **124-25** *ph* Christopher Drake/Eva Johnson's house in Suffolk, interiors designed by Eva Johnson; **125a** *ph* Debi Treloar/Mark and Sally of Baileys Home and Garden's house in Herefordshire; **125b** *ph* Debi Treloar/Debi Treloar's home in London; **126-27** *ph* Debi Treloar; **127** *ph* Pia Tryde/the garden of Vanessa de Lisle, fashion consultant, London; **128** *ph* David Brittain; **129l** *ph* Christopher Drake; **129c** *ph* Christopher Drake/owners of La Cour Beaudeval Antiquities, Mireille and Jean Claude Lothon's house in Faverolles; **129r** *ph* Christopher Drake/Eva Johnson's house in Suffolk, interiors designed by Eva Johnson; **130l** *ph* Melanie Eclare/Fiona Naylor and Peter Marlow's roof garden in London designed by Fiona Naylor and landscape architect Lindsey Whitelaw; **130c** *ph* Pia Tryde; **130r** *ph* Christopher Drake; **131l** *ph* Christopher Drake/linen cushion, L'Utile e il Dilettevole; **131r** *ph* Nicki Dowey/deckchairs from Crocus; **132 both** *ph* Melanie Eclare/Mirabel Osler's garden in Ludlow, Shropshire; **133a** *ph* Melanie Eclare/Laura Cooper & Nick Taggart's Los Angeles garden designed by Cooper/Taggart Designs; **133b** *ph* Christopher Drake/Eva Johnson's house in Suffolk, interiors designed by Eva Johnson; **134a** *ph* Christopher Drake; **134cl** *ph* Melanie Eclare/Sarah Harrison & Jamie Hodder-Williams's roof terrace in London designed by Stephen Woodhams; **134cr** *ph* Melanie Eclare/garden designed by Judy Kameon, Elysian Landscapes; **134bl** *ph* Melanie Eclare/Carol Valentine's garden in California, designed by Isabelle Greene, F.A.S.L.A., a California landscape architect and planner; **134br** *ph* Melanie Eclare; **135a all** *ph* Christopher Drake; **135cl** *ph* Melanie Eclare/Nancy Goslee Power, garden designer; **135c** *ph* Melanie Eclare/a house in Chelsea, lighting designed by Sally Storey; **135cr** *ph* Catherine Gratwicke/Peter Adler's house & gallery in London; **135b** *ph* Pia Tryde; **136a** *ph* Chris Everard/Pemper and Rabiner home in New York, designed by David Khouri of Comma; **136b** *ph* Christopher Drake; **136a** *ph* David Brittain; **137bl** *ph* Christopher Drake/Enrica Stabile's house in Brunello; **137br** *ph* Christopher Drake/Diane Bauer's house near Cotignac.

business credits

key: *ph*= photographer, **a**=above, **b**=below, **r**=right, **l**=left, **c**=centre.

www.63hlg.com
Pages 12–13, 40, 78–79,
109r.

ANDERSON ARCHITECTS
555 West 25th Street
New York, NY 10001
USA
+ 1 212 620 0996
www.andersonarch.com
Page 15.

ANGELA A'COURT
orangedawe@hotmail.com
Pages 71al, 113b.

ANGELA SOUTHWELL
interior designer
01732 763246
angsouthwell@hotmail.com
Page 91.

ASH SAKULA ARCHITECTS
24 Rosebery Avenue
London EC1R 4SX
020 7837 9735
www.ashsak.com
Pages 61br, 70bl.

ASPLUND
showroom and shop:
Sibyllegatan 31
114 42 Stockholm
Sweden
+ 46 8 662 52 84
Page 12l.

AZMAN ASSOCIATES
(formerly Azman Owens
Architects)
18 Charlotte Road
London EC2A 3PB
020 7739 8191
www.azmanarchitects.com
Page 100a.

BAILEYS HOME & GARDEN
01989 563015
www.baileys
homeandgarden.com
Page 125a.

BEHUN/ZIFF DESIGN
153 E. 53rd Street
43rd Floor
New York, NY 10022
USA
+ 1 212 292 6233
Page 110l.

BONNIE YOUNG
+ 1 212 228 0832
Page 112r.

BOOKWORKS
34 Ansleigh Place
London W11 4BW
020 7792 8310
Page 53 inset.

BRUNO TANQUEREL
2 Passage St Sébastien
75011 Paris, France
+ 33 1 43 57 03 93
Page 112bl.

CARDEN CUNIETTI
83 Westbourne Park Road
London W2 5QH
office: 020 7229 8559
shop: 020 7229 8630
www.carden-cunietti.com
Page 39ar.

CARNACHAN ARCHITECTS
33 Bath Street
PO Box 37–717, Parnell
Auckland
New Zealand
+ 64 9 3797 234
Pages 47c, 69l.

CHARLES BATESON DESIGN
CONSULTANTS
18 Kings Road
St Margaret's
Twickenham TW1 2QS
020 8892 3141
charles.bateson@
btinternet.com
Pages 35l, 64r.

CHESTER JONES
240 Battersea Park Road
London SW11 4NG
020 7498 2717
chester.jones@virgin.net
Page 89.

CHRISTINA WILSON
christinawilson@
btopenworld.com
Pages 77r, 81l, 120b.

CHRISTOPHER LEACH DESIGN
07765 255566
mail@christopherleach.com
Page 17.

CLARE MOSLEY
020 7708 3123
Pages 25br, 72c.

CLIVE BUTCHER DESIGNS
The Granary
The Quay, Wivenhoe
Essex CO7 9BU
01206 827 708
Page 112al.

COBURN ARCHITECTURE
45 Main Street
Suite 1210
Brooklyn, NY 11201
USA
+ 1 718 624 1700
www.coburnarch.com
Page 114l.

COLIN ORCHARD DESIGN
219a Kings Road
London SW3 5EJ
020 7352 2116
Pages 6, 43a.

CONSTANZE VON UNRUH
Constanze Interior Projects
020 8948 5533
www.constanze
interiorprojects.com
Page 47r.

COOPER/TAGGART DESIGNS
+ 1 323 254 3048
coopertaggart@earthlink.net
Page 133a.

COSKUN FINE ART LONDON
93 Walton Street
London SW3 2HP
020 7581 9056
www.coskunfineart.com
Page 122.

CR STUDIO ARCHITECTS, PC
6 West 18th Street, 9th Floor
New York, NY 10011
USA
+ 1 212 989 8187
www.crstudio.com
Page 88l.

D–SQUARED DESIGN
6b Blackbird Yard
Ravenscroft Street
London E2 7RP
020 7739 2632
dsquared@globalnet.co.uk
Page 88r.

DANIELA MICOL WAJSKOL
Via Vincenzo Monti 42
20123 Milan, Italy
daniela.w@tiscalinet.it
Page 11l, 23, 123l.

DAVID KHOURI
Comma
149 Wooster Street
Suite 4NW
New York, NY 10012
USA
+ 1 212 420 7866
www.comma-nyc.com
Page 136a.

DAVID MIKHAIL ARCHITECTS
Unit 29
1–13 Adler Street
London E1 1EE
020 7377 8424
www.davidmikhail.com
Page 118r.

DEBI TRELOAR
www.debitreloar.com
Page 4–5, 72br, 125b.

DIDIER GOMEZ
Ory Gomez
15 rue Henri Heine
75016 Paris
France
+ 33 01 44 30 8823
orygomez@free.fr
Pages 16–17, 29, 76 inset.

DIRAND JOSEPH
ARCHITECTURE
338 rue des Pyrenees
75020 Paris
France
+ 33 01 47 97 78 57
joseph.dirand@wanadoo.fr
Page 77al.

ELENA COLOMBO
eacolombo@earthlink.net
Page 39c.

EMMA WILSON
photographic shoots:
www.45crossleyst.com
holiday lets in Morocco:
www.castlesinthesand.com
Pages 19c, 42bl, 63r.

EMILY CHALMERS
Caravan
11 Lamb Street, Spitalfields
London E1 6EA
020 7247 6467
www.emilychalmers.com
Pages 120a, 121al.

ENRICA STABILE
L'Utile e il Dilettevole
Via Carlo Maria Maggi 6
20154 Milan, Italy
+ 39 0234 53 60 86
www.enricastabile.com
Pages 7ar, 22r, 137bl.

EVA JOHNSON
01638 731 362
www.evajohnson.com
**Pages 121ar, 124–125, 129r,
133b.**

FILIP VAN BEVER
Filipvanbever@skynet.be
Page 53 main.

HELEN ELLERY
The Plot London
77 Compton Street
London EC1V 0BN
020 7251 8116
www.theplotlondon.com
Page 75r.

HENRI FITZWILLIAM-LAY
hfitz@hotmail.com
Page 100bl.

HER HOUSE
30d Great Sutton Street
London EC1V 0DS
020 7689 0606/0808
www.herhouse.uk.com
Page 11r.

INTERIOR CONCEPTS
6 Warren Hall
Manor Road
Loughton
Essex IG10 4RP
020 8508 9952
www.jointeriorconcepts.co.uk
Page 50l.

IPL INTERIORS
25 Bullen Street
London SW11 3ER
020 7978 4224
Page 118l.

ISABELLE C. GREENE, FASLA
2613 De La Vina Street
Santa Barbara, CA 93105
USA
+ 1 805 569 4045
icgreene@aol.com
Page 134bl.

J&M DAVIDSON
gallery:
97 Golborne Road
London W10 5NL
shop:
42 Ledbury Road
London W11 2SE
Page 74.

JACKSON'S
5 All Saint's Road
London W11 1HA
020 7792 8336
Page 85l.

JACOMINI INTERIOR DESIGN
1701 Brun Street, Suite 101
Houston, TX 77019
USA
+ 1 713 524 8224
www.jacominidesign.com
Page 99a.

JAMIE FALLA
MOOArc
198 Blackstock Road
London N5 1EN
www.mooarc.com
Pages 51r, 68r.

JEFFREY BILHUBER
Bilhuber Inc
330 East 59th Street
6th Floor
New York, NY 10022
USA
+ 1 212 308 4888
Page 119b.

JENNIFER POST DESIGN
390 W. End Avenue
New York, NY 10024
USA
+ 1 212 769 0338
Page 39br.

JOANN BARWICK INTERIORS
PO Box 982
Boca Grande, FL 33921
USA
Page 105b.

J.O.B. INTERIEUR
Dijkstraat 5
3961 AA Wijk bij Duurstede
The Netherlands
+ 31 343 578818
JOBINT@xs4all.nl
Page 103b.

JOHN BARMAN INC.
500 Park Avenue
New York, NY 10022
USA
+ 1 212 838 9443
www.johnbarman.com
Page 59b, 65l.

JOHN C HOPE ARCHITECTS
3 St Bernards Crescent
Edinburgh EH4 1NR
0131 315 2215
Page 101cl.

JOHNSON-NAYLOR INTERIOR
ARCHITECTURE
020 7490 8885
www.johnsonnaylor.com
Page 130l.

JONATHAN CLARK
ARCHITECTS
020 7286 5676
jonathan@jonathanclarkarchit
ects.co.uk
Page 48.

JONATHAN REED
Reed Creative Services
151a Sydney Street
London SW3 6NT
020 7565 0066
Page 67l.

JOSEPHINE RYAN
63 Abbeville Road
London SW4 9JW
020 8675 3900
Page 19r.

JUDY KAMEON
Elysian Landscapes
724 Academy Road
Los Angeles, CA 90012
USA
+ 1 323 226 9588
www.plainair.com
Page 134cr.

JWFLOWERS.COM
Unit E8 & 9
1–45 Durham Street
London SE11 5JH
020 7735 7771
www.jwflowers.com
Page 75a.

KAREN NICOL
020 8979 4593
karenicol@hotmail.com
Page 37cl

KARIM RASHID INC.
357 W. 17th Street
New York, NY 10011
USA
+ 1 212 929 8657
www.karimrashid.com
Page 51b

KEN FOREMAN
105 Duane Street
New York, NY 10007
USA
+ 1 212 924 4503
Pages 8l, 31b, 32

KRISTIINA RATIA DESIGNS
+ 1 203 852 0027
Pages 118–19.

MIREILLE AND
JEAN-CLAUDE LOTHON
LA COUR BEAUDEVAL
ANTIQUITIES
4 rue des Fontaines
28210 Faverolles
France
+ 33 2 37 51 47 67
Page 129c.

LAURENT BAYARD INTERIORS
020 7328 2022
Page 37cr.

LISA BYNON GARDEN
DESIGN
PO Box 897
Sag Harbor, NY 11963
USA
+ 1 631 725 4680
Page 28l.

LOUISE ROBBINS
Insideout House and Garden
Agency and
Malt House Bed & Breakfast
01544 340681
lulawrence1@aol.com
Pages 71ac, 72bl, 98.

MAISONETTE
79 Chamberlayne Road
London NW10 3ND
020 8964 8444
www.maisonette.uk.com
Page 10, 70br.

MARC MEIRÉ
Meirefamily@aol.com
Pages 44–45.

MARK SMITH AT
SMITHCREATIVE
15 St Georges Road
London W4 1AU
020 8747 3909
mark@smithcreative.net
Page 77bl.

MCLEAN QUINLAN
ARCHITECTS
2a Bellevue Parade
London SW17 7EQ
020 8767 1633
www.mcleanquinlan.com
Pages 82-83.

MONA NERENBERG
BLOOM
43 Madison Street
Sag Harbor, NY 11963
USA
+ 1 631 725 4680
Page 28l.

MONEO BROCK STUDIO
Francisco de Asis Mendez
Casariego 7, Bajo
28002 Madrid
Spain
+ 34 91 563 8056
www.moneobrock.com
Pages 56a, 59a.

MULLMAN SEIDMAN
ARCHITECTS
443 Greenwich Street, # 2A
New York, NY 10013
USA
+ 1 212 431 0770
www.mullmanseidman.com
**Pages 13b, 25, 49r, 58a, 62,
66-67, 67r, 115 main.**

NANCY GOSLEE POWER &
ASSOCIATES
1660 Stanford Street
Santa Monica, CA 90904
USA
+ 1 310 264 0266
ngpa@nancypower.com
Page 135cl.

NICO RENSCH
ARCHITEAM
www.architeam.co.uk
Pages 38b, 39bl.

NORDIC STYLE
109 Lots Road
London SW10 0RN
020 7351 1755
www.nordicstyle.com
Page 102b.

PATERSON GORNALL
INTERIORS
50 Lavender Gardens
London SW11 1DN
020 7738 2530
Page 112al.

PETER ADLER
020 7262 1775
Page 135cr.

SIMON KIMMINS DESIGN AND
PROJECT CONTROL
020 8314 1526
Page 14l.

ROGER OATES DESIGN
01531 632718
www.rogeroates.co.uk
Pages 41a, 43b, 46, 94.

RÜTZOU A/S
+ 45 35240616
www.rutzou.com
Page 30-31

SALLY STOREY
John Cullen Lighting
585 Kings Road
London SW6 2EH
020 7371 5400
Pages 67l, 135c.

SASHA GIBB
01534 863211
home@sashagibb.co.uk
Page 36ar.

SETH STEIN
15 Grand Union Centre
West Row
Ladbroke Grove
London W10 5AS
020 8968 8581
www.sethstein.com
Page 113a.

SHARLAND & LEWIS
52 Long Street
Tetbury
Gloucester GL8 8AQ
01666 500354
www.sharlandandlewis.com
Pages 7bl, 56b.

SIAN COLLEY SOFT
FURNISHINGS
Block E 2B Upper Ringway
Bounds Green
London N11 2UD
020 8368 4092
colleysian@hotmail.com
Page 39al.

SIMON COLEBROOK OF THE
DOUGLAS STEPHEN
PARTNERSHIP
DS Property & Landscaping
Services
34 Rockwood Crescent
Hucknall
Nottingham NG15 6PY
www.dspl.co.uk
Page 81r.

SIMON CONDER ASSOCIATES
Nile Street Studios
8 Nile Street
London N1 7RF
020 7251 2144
www.simonconder.co.uk
Page 114r.

SOPHIE EADIE
The New England Shutter Co.
16 Jaggard Way
London SW12 8SG
020 8675 1099
www.tnesc.co.uk
Page 97r.

STEPHEN VARADY
Architecture
PO Box 105
St Peters
NSW 2044
Australia
+ 61 2 9516 4044
Page 50r.

STEPHEN WOODHAMS
Unit 3
McKay Trading Estate
248-300 Kensal Road
London W10 5BZ
020 8964 9818
Page 134cl.

STICKLAND COOMBE
258 Lavender Hill
London SW11 1LJ
020 7924 1699
www.sticklandcoombe.com
**Pages 51l, 54-55, 103a, 111
inset.**

STUDIO WORKS
6775 Centinela Avenue
Building # 3
Culver City, CA 90230
USA
+ 1 301 390 5051
Page 119a.

TESSUTI
Doorniksewijk 76
8500 Kortrijk
Belgium
+ 32 56 25 29 27
www.tessuti.be
Pages 53 main, 100br.

TOTEM DESIGN
IAN HUME
2 Alexander Street
London W2 5NT
020 7243 0692
totem.uk@virgin.net
Page 100bl.

URBAN RESEARCH LAB
www.smcurbanlab.com
Page 111 main

VICENTE WOLF ASSOCIATES
333 West 39th Street
Suite 1001
New York, NY 10018
USA
+ 1 212 465 0590
Page 33b.

VOON WONG & BENSON SAW
Unit 27, 1 Stannary Street
London SE11 4AD
020 7587 0116
www.voon-benson.com
Page 41b.

WALLENSTEEN & CO AB
Floragatan 11
114 31 Stockholm
Sweden
+ 46 8 210151
wallensteen@chello.se
Page 28r.

WHITELAW TURKINGTON
Landscape Architects
020 7820 0388
Page 130l.

WILLIAM YEOWARD
270 Kings Road
London SW3 5AW
020 7349 7828
www.williamyeoward.com
Pages 6, 43a.

YVES-CLAUDE DESIGN
Architectural/industrial design
firm specializing in stainless-
steel kitchens, furniture and
interiors
199 Lafayette Street
New York, NY 10012
USA
www.kanso.com
Pages 55a, 61ar, 63l, 69r.

index